STUDIES IN INTERNATIONAL SECURITY

*

STUDIES IN INTERNATIONAL SECURITY: 10

DEFEATING COMMUNIST INSURGENCY

The Lessons of Malaya and Vietnam

Sir Robert Thompson

FREDERICK A. PRAEGER, *Publishers*

New York • Washington

BOOKS THAT MATTER

Published in the United States of America in 1966
by Frederick A. Praeger, Inc., Publishers
111 Fourth Avenue, New York, N.Y. 10003

Printed in the United States of America

This book is dedicated to those men and women in Asia who, in every walk of life, have accepted the call of leadership in the fight against communism, and have given up their lives in the strong faith and expectation that others will have the courage to take their place.

CONTENTS

MAPS

Preface

This book on counter-insurgency is based on my experiences of the Emergency in Malaya from 1948 to 1960, and of the three and a half years which I spent in South Vietnam from September 1961 to March 1965 as Head of the British Advisory Mission. It is not intended in any sense to be a history of the insurgencies in either country. Nor is it intended to provide an analysis of the present situation and prospects in South Vietnam in the summer of 1965. I have endeavoured to set out, for the benefit of the layman, both the theory of insurgency as applied on the ground in both countries by a communist insurgent movement, and what I consider to be the basic theory of counter-insurgency as it should be applied to defeat the threat in those and similar situations.

I do not claim that the book is complete. It is no more than a contribution which may help the newsreader to understand, amidst all the day-to-day reporting of incidents, what is happening on the ground and what governments coping with an insurgency should be attempting to do. It may also provide the professional with a framework around which to build a fuller study of all aspects of counter-insurgency, which must inevitably vary according to terrain and the conditions prevailing in a threatened country at any given time. I have purposely avoided much of the operational detail, and have made only one reference to the many other works on the subject. I have also tried to avoid the jargon, and have even resisted the temptation to include a glossary of terms not used, having been completely foxed from the outset in an attempt to define that hard-worked term 'motivation'.

If I had to produce a bibliography, it would be headed by a book which no one else would include: *The Man-Eating Leopard of Rudraprayag* (Oxford University Press, 1947) by the late Jim Corbett (and his *Man-Eaters of Kumaon*, Oxford

University Press, 1944). This provides an excellent example of a vast area of countryside under the terrorist control of a man-eating leopard, showing the effect on the lives of the people and of the pilgrims who passed through the area, and describes the painstaking methods required to deal with the threat. My list would also include Philip Woodruff's *The Men Who Ruled India* (Jonathan Cape, 1953 and 1954, 2 vols.). This contains a wealth of human and government experience gained in the administration of rural agricultural communities, which in itself is the root of the problem. From this it should be clear to the reader that the bias of this book is heavily weighted on the administrative and other aspects of an insurgency rather than the military. If the reader wants the tactics and the blood and guts of guerilla operations, there are plenty of good books on the subject and there will be many more.

Nor is this book complete in another sense. In neither Malaysia nor Vietnam have we yet seen the end of the struggle. We are witnessing in the 1960s a new development in insurgency of armed interference by neighbouring countries in support of next-door subversive and insurgent movements on a scale which would in the past have been termed aggression and have led to war, but which is now classified as 'seepage', 'infiltration' or 'incursion'. This in turn has led in Vietnam to 'retaliation' or the 'measured response' by the South Vietnamese and American Air Forces against North Vietnam. No one can yet assess the significance of these developments, or the part which they will play in deciding the final result of an insurgency. They are not in any book—not even one by Mao Tse-tung!

This book, therefore, should not be viewed out of context. It is not related to the current situations in either Malaysia or Vietnam, though certain parts of it could still be applicable. It may show how such situations have arisen, and if it helps to show how the present situation in Vietnam can be prevented elsewhere, it will have served its purpose.

I owe a great debt of gratitude to my colleagues in the British Advisory Mission for their help in developing the concepts contained in this book, and for the encouragement which they and many others gave me to record them. I am also very grateful to Miss Rosemary Spencer, my secretary during the last few months in Saigon, for devoting so much of her spare time there, and on leave afterwards, to typing the first and final drafts of the manuscript.

I am indebted, too, to the Controller of Her Majesty's Stationery Office for permission to quote excerpts from official documents of the British Advisory Mission which are Crown Copyright.

Finally, I must state that the views and opinions expressed in this book are my own and not necessarily those of any government with which I have been associated.

Winsford, Somerset   ROBERT THOMPSON
July 1965

SOUTH-EAST ASIA

Chapter 1

The Setting

'THE only person who really understands communism is the communist who understands it too late'—just, in fact, as he is about to be disembowelled, garrotted or, more mercifully, shot by his former comrades. His crime may have been revisionism, deviationism, suspected treachery or one of many others which rate a summary death penalty for those who are engaged in a 'People's Revolutionary War' and become disillusioned with the cause or plain exhausted with the protracted struggle.

This quotation is one of the better phrases to have come out of Vietnam and pinpoints the following question: What is the appeal of communism in south-east Asian communities, and why are young men in particular attracted to its cause? But the two further questions more worrying to the Westerner, cosy in his free and increasingly affluent society, are these: How do communist guerilla forces survive, and even threaten to prevail over, large-scale conventional forces supported by countries whose power, wealth and good intentions are seemingly invincible? And, above all, how can they be defeated except at enormous cost in men, money, material and time and without risk of general war?

The answers to the first two questions are by no means conclusive, even to those who have studied the works of Mao Tse-tung and Vo Nguyen Giap, and the answer to the third is being learnt the hard way. To study some of the lessons from Malaya and Vietnam, it is first necessary to consider the background and effects of the Second World War.

*　　*　　*

Although there were earlier indigenous movements in both Indonesia and Indo-China, communism in south-east Asia received its main impetus in the 1920s from China, where the

Far Eastern Bureau of the Comintern had been established in Shanghai. Its chief disciples were Chinese immigrants, who during this period were leaving China in large numbers to seek their fortunes in the developing south-east Asian colonies and protectorates of the British, French and Dutch. In the first instance the targets of these communist cadres were mainly students in Chinese schools and Chinese labour employed in the ports and on rubber estates and tin mines. Only in Vietnam did they succeed in penetrating nationalist political movements which were already formed amongst the Vietnamese in opposition to the French colonial power. Communism itself was outlawed and illegal and therefore developed slowly, using the well-known cell system to expand its membership. In the 1930s it was able to gain a certain notoriety and support amongst the overseas Chinese community by sponsoring movements designed to bolster Chinese nationalist opposition to the Japanese invasion of China.

Even so, communism was no real threat to the security of the colonial governments or to the well-being of the peoples of south-east Asia in the period immediately before the Second World War. It was the war which established communism as a major force in the area. With the Japanese occupation of French Indo-China and the defeat of the British in Malaya, culminating in the fall of Singapore in early 1942, the communists alone retained any organization within the population capable of offering further resistance to the Japanese. At the same time the earlier German attack on Russia, as a result of which Russia became a Western ally, gave to communism a label of respectability which it had not previously enjoyed. As a result, the communists were rapidly able to gain control over the popular resistance movements to the Japanese and became wartime allies of the West. As such, both in Indo-China and in Malaya, they were supported by the South-East Asia Command, and were able to build up reasonably strong armed units in these territories. Many weapons had already been salvaged from the battlefields, and more were supplied in the later stages of the war by long-range air supply drops. (In Malaya those weapons which landed on the organized drop sites, and which were listed by British liaison officers as issued to the resistance movement, were handed back on disbandment at the end of the war, but many supply drops went astray.) More important, the communist parties in control of the resistance movements were able to expand their control and influence through all sections of the population hostile to the Japanese, and, in Malaya for example, the Malayan People's Anti-Japanese Union embraced most of the Chinese population in the Malayan Peninsula and in Singapore.

With the defeat of Japan and before Allied troops could arrive, the resistance forces were for a time in almost total control of the territories, during which period they took the opportunity to eliminate not only many of those who had collaborated with the Japanese, but also many others who might be expected to oppose communism in the future. The communist parties in both territories therefore came out of the war in a strong position and were able to make capital out of many of the side-effects of the war itself.

They could point to the ignominious defeats of the British and French by an Asian power over which they themselves claimed the final victory in the territories concerned. They also had behind them the great reputation earned by Russia for the defence of the motherland and the ultimate defeat of the German armies in eastern Europe. This backing by Russia was later to be enhanced by the backing of China, when Mao Tse-tung and the Chinese Communist armies ultimately defeated Chiang Kai-shek and the Nationalist armies in 1950.

Another effect of the war and of the immediate post-war era was the awakening of the Asian rural population to the modern world in general. During the war many of the remotest areas had been penetrated by troops of different countries; millions of people had seen aircraft and been subjected to political propaganda from one side or the other for the first time. There was a growing awareness that, with the end of the war and the defeat of Japan, there could be no return to the conditions of the pre-war colonial era.

The post-war situation was inevitably chaotic, more so in Vietnam than in Malaya. In Vietnam, which was temporarily re-occupied by the British in the South and the Nationalist

Chinese in the North, it was some time before the French forces returned and before the French administration could regain control of any portion of the country. The French were faced with an immediate guerilla war against the Viet Minh, now fully under the control of the communist Lao Dong (Workers) Party. In Malaya, the British re-occupation forces were too strong for the Malayan Communist Party to oppose militarily, and the Party therefore agreed to disband its armed units in return for certain concessions, most important of which was that it should be recognized as a legal political party. In this role it hoped to be able to exploit the political and economic changes which resulted from the war. It had some success in capturing the young and growing trade-union movement, in spite of the patient and courageous efforts of a few trade-union experts sent out by the post-war Labour government in Britain. It also made some headway among students in Chinese schools, and in promoting or penetrating various popular associations and left-wing political parties. It made little appeal, however, as a political party on its own, and as the country recovered administratively and economically from the war, it started to lose ground. It was decided, therefore, to revert to the 'armed struggle', and in June 1948 what came to be called 'the Emergency' broke out in Malaya. It was to last twelve years, until July 1960, three years after the Federation of Malaya became independent.

The Emergency can be divided into three broad phases: the first was a build-up period on both sides, during which government policies were formulated and the necessary initial measures taken. This period culminated in the murder of Sir Henry Gurney, High Commissioner at that time, and the appointment of General (later Field-Marshal) Sir Gerald Templer as High Commissioner and Director of Operations. The second phase, from 1952 to 1954, saw the success of the measures taken and the military defeat of the insurgents. This period ended with the abortive peace talks at Baling in 1955 that had been set in motion by peace feelers from the Malayan Communist Party. The final period of five years was devoted to the mopping-up of the remaining communist terrorist gangs, at the end of which the last remnants, numbering little more

than five hundred, took refuge in the jungles astride the
Malaya-Thailand frontier, where they have remained in
dwindling numbers to this day.

In Indo-China the Viet Minh war against the French
ended, after the French defeat at Dien Bien Phu, with the
Geneva Agreement of 1954, which divided Vietnam into the
communist North and the free and independent South, where
Ngo Dinh Diem became Prime Minister and subsequently, on
the declaration of a Republic, the first President. Much to
everyone's surprise he survived the troubles and difficulties of
the first few years and gradually restored law and order and a
degree of prosperity to the country. Thwarted in their hope
that South Vietnam would be united with the North either
by elections or by chaos, the government in Hanoi realized
that their aims could only be achieved through insurgency.
This broke out openly in the Mekong Delta in 1959 and was
gradually extended throughout the whole of South Vietnam.
It has been raging bitterly ever since.

It is with this war against the Viet Cong in South Vietnam
and with the Emergency in Malaya that this book is concerned.

*   *   *

Both Malaya and South Vietnam have much in common,
and it may be useful at this point to list some of their simi-
larities and differences. Both are tropical and subject to heavy
rainfall, which is more persistent throughout the year in
Malaya, resulting in thicker vegetation, which makes the
Malayan jungle more inaccessible. South Vietnam is more
than one and a half times the size of Malaya, being approximately 750 miles long, compared with Malaya's 500. Neither
country is much wider at any point than 100 miles. Both
countries have a central mountain range rising to over 5,000
feet, nearly all of which is covered in dense jungle.

Both countries are mainly agricultural and of recent
development, with the emphasis in Malaya on cash crops such
as rubber and rather less on rice, of which she produces only
about two-thirds of her annual requirements, whereas in

Vietnam the main emphasis is on rice and a great deal less on cash crops. The Mekong Delta is probably the richest rice land in the world, and South Vietnam in normal years would be one of the main rice exporters. Malaya has the added advantage of tin and iron ore, and is the world's largest producer of both natural rubber and tin. Whereas South Vietnam compared with many Asian countries is relatively prosperous on the basis of subsistence agriculture, Malaya is far more prosperous economically and financially, even though the population of South Vietnam (about fourteen millions) is double that of Malaya and Singapore (about seven millions). For example, total Vietnamese imports and exports in 1960 were valued at under US $150 millions, whereas the equivalent Malayan figure (excluding Singapore) was US $1,700 millions—more than ten times greater. One effect of this wealth is that the populated areas of Malaya are more highly developed, with good roads and communications, whereas many of the populated areas in Vietnam are comparatively inaccessible; there are few all-weather roads in Vietnam, transport depending in the heavily populated and more highly developed Mekong Delta south of Saigon almost entirely on the waterways.

Another result of the different form of development is that the rural population of Vietnam is composed of peasants—approximately twelve millions—whereas in Malaya the number of peasants, predominantly Malaya, is about half the rural population, the remaining half being composed of estate and mine labour, mainly Chinese and Indian.

Without going into the merits or demerits of the French and British colonial administrative systems (or the disadvantage from which the French suffered at the end of the war), a far greater advance had been made in Malaya in establishing a Malayan administration and in training local officers to fill it. Moreover, during the first years of the Emergency, including the vital period between 1952 and 1954, there was still a strong executive British element in the administration and, constitutionally, final decisions rested with a British High Commissioner. The British role was therefore very different from the advisory role enjoyed by the Americans in Vietnam in support of a government which was already independent.

We have, then, a Malaya in comparison smaller, more prosperous and better administered: all great advantages in counter-insurgency. But perhaps the greatest advantage of all was that Malaya was completely isolated from outside communist support, having only a 150-mile frontier with friendly Thailand in the north (with whom there was a border agreement under which Malayan police forces could operate across the border) and a 1,000-mile sea coast which could easily be patrolled. In Vietnam, by contrast, there was on the west a long land frontier bordering on Laos and Cambodia and twisting for about 900 miles, at least two-thirds of it through undeveloped jungle areas, and on the east an even longer coastline easily accessible to small-boat and junk traffic. Across the short northern border, at the 17th parallel, lay the communist North in a position to take full advantage of this weakness.

To offset this, South Vietnam had a number of advantages on the outbreak of insurgency. Her people had experienced the Viet Minh war against the French, and many nationalists who had fought with the Viet Minh were now on the government side. The peasants in many areas had had a taste of communist rule and were now beginning to reap the first benefits of the government's land development and land reform policies. This general advantage was reinforced by the strong core of anti-communist refugees from the North (more than 800,000—mainly Roman Catholics). There was also a dedicated and determined leadership not solely confined to the Ngo family. This local leadership had to be built up in Malaya during the Emergency, and local leaders had to prove themselves.

Further, the Vietnamese were dealing with their own people, whereas in Malaya a mainly British and Malay government and its forces were dealing with an insurgent movement which was 90 per cent Chinese and depended for its support on the Chinese rural population. While this gave the government an advantage in the Malay areas of the country, great care was necessary to avoid Sino-Malay racial incidents, and a major political effort was required to convince the bulk of the Chinese population that they had a stake in Malaya as Malayans and not as Chinese with the communists.

Finally, South Vietnam enjoyed almost unlimited support from the American government. A Vietnamese army of seven divisions (about 150,000) was already in existence. Malaya had two battalions, increased by the end of the Emergency to nine. These were supplemented by British Commonwealth units and battalions, which were constantly changing and which at their greatest strength (there were other commitments such as Korea and Kenya) did not number more than twenty-five in both Malaya and Singapore. The highest army strength, including supporting elements and headquarters, was a little over 20,000 in 1951. Other British aid, including finance, was marginal, and in Malaya much depended on the crafty use of a 'shoe-string', never a feature of American aid.

Whatever the differences, however, the enemy was exactly the same, being represented in Malaya by the Malayan Communist Party and by its military counterpart, the Malayan Races Liberation Army, commonly referred to as the Communist Terrorists (CTs), and in Vietnam by the Lao Dong (Workers) Party, subsequently to be camouflaged behind the National Front for the Liberation of South Vietnam, and by its military counterpart, commonly referred to as the Viet Cong (VC).

Chapter 2

Communist Subversion

THE Second World War, then, and its aftermath, gave the Communist Parties in both countries the opportunity to build up strength based on the resistance movements to the Japanese and to collect an initial stock of weapons with which to arm their guerilla units. We must now consider the causes on which the communist insurgency was based.

Every insurgency, particularly a communist revolutionary one, requires a cause. Resistance to the Japanese was no longer valid, but it had given an air of respectability to the Communist Party, which was a valuable heritage not to be lightly discarded. For this reason every effort was made to adopt causes which appeared legitimate, progressive and desirable. The basic cause was ready to hand: anti-colonialism. It was on this that the Emergency was based and also the war against the French in Indo-China. It did not quite fit the situation prevailing in South Vietnam after 1954, but by twisting the cause to anti-imperialism it could be made to apply to the United States' presence in South Vietnam at the invitation of and in support of the Ngo Dinh Diem government.

Given a basic cause, many other issues can be tacked onto it, such as land for the landless, exploitation of labour on estates and mines, regional autonomy for ethnic minorities and political equality for immigrant races with the indigenous races. At the same time, all local seeds of conflict within a community can be exploited, as between young and old, between progressive and traditional, between different religions and races, and even between local capitalists and foreign capitalists. There is always some issue which has an appeal to each section of the community, and, even if dormant, an inspired incident may easily revive it in an acute form. This particularly applies during the course of the insurgency itself, when new causes can be developed from events, and, if necessary, old ones be forgotten. For example, the dominant cause in Vietnam in the summer of 1965 is to drive the American forces out. The fact that, but for the insurgency, they would not have been there can be conveniently ignored. It is simple enough to confuse cause and effect. You can also stick your Aunt Sally up in order to knock it down.

All governments are vulnerable to criticism, and every grievance, shortcoming or abuse will be exploited. Waste in government expenditure, failure to fulfil promises and the incidence of taxation are just as lively issues in the east as in the west, and even more so in remote rural communities, where the tax collector and the policeman are the central government's more prominent representatives. (When the insurgents gain control over such areas, they are careful to reduce taxes on land and crops well below the government level or even to remit them for a period. This they can afford to do, having no overheads, and still not lack for money.) Corruption is always another credible charge and rarely fails to stick.

It is the whole purpose of the appeal that it should be directed to all sections of the community and for this reason it is normally phrased in unexceptionable terms. It is worth giving in full the manifesto of the National Front for the Liberation of South Vietnam, which was summarized in a broadcast from Hanoi in April 1962, calling for the overthrow of President Diem and the formation of a broad national democratic administration in South Vietnam. The Front promised to

(1) release all political prisoners unconditionally;

(2) guarantee freedom to all mass organizations and parties;

(3) carry out freedom of opinion and the Press;

(4) abrogate the constitution and dissolve the National Assembly;

(5) hold elections for a new Assembly with a 'democratic spirit', which would decide on the nature and form of the regime;

(6) eliminate the American trade monopoly and accept economic and technical aid from all countries;

(7) learn from the culture of all countries, regardless of political regime;

(8) secure a policy of neutrality by opening diplomatic relations with all countries (in conformity with the Bandung Principles), avoiding a military alliance with any country; and

(9) advance peaceful reunification.

A similar manifesto was issued by the Malayan Communist Party at the beginning of the Emergency, including reunification with Singapore, which was then a separate government. The reader will be struck by the vagueness of the internal platform and the failure to define too closely what is meant by 'freedom' and a 'democratic spirit'. It should be particularly noted that the word 'communism' does not appear at all; even the communists realize that it is a dirty word. Nor do they take a chance on 'socialism'.

In furtherance of these aims, the Front undertook to unite people of 'all strata, classes, nationalities, political parties, mass organizations, religious communities and patriotic personalities in South Vietnam'. All they needed in common was to be 'against the United States imperialists and their henchmen'.

But above all the communist appeal is directed to youth. For the intellectual there is the ideological appeal of communism; for the uneducated there is the appeal of change. The rural youth of Asia was no longer prepared to accept the humdrum existence of village rural life, where the most he could expect was to succeed his father on a small plot of land. The desire to escape from this rut was closely allied with a desire for further education, so that he could take his place in a modern and progressive community. Stated in one phrase, communism appeared to offer the cheapest and quickest passport to modernity.

Whereas this may have been true for the post-war decade, it is an interesting aside to consider whether communism does not now appeal as the only alternative to modernization in a world which is becoming so highly technical. Few, if any, underdeveloped countries can hope to keep pace with the advances of the western world. There will therefore be a temptation to seek the curtain of isolation which communism provides, and behind which an illusion of progress along a different path can be maintained, when in fact there will be stagnation (as in Cuba).

In their approach to youth the communists make it clear that the revolution will be a long and arduous struggle. This is underlined by the example of China, where it took forty years to achieve victory. When times are hard and food is perhaps short, the inevitability of final victory has always been a strong card to play. The promised land can be made to look brighter the further it is away.

Given all these ingredients, the witches' brew is strong enough to inspire an insurgency but is still not sufficiently potent to get it actually off the ground. One other practical factor is required, and that is a breakdown, or near breakdown, of the government's rural administration. In Malaya this factor was provided by the vast number of Chinese squatters who, during the Japanese occupation when there was a large measure of unemployment, moved out into the remoter valleys of the country, mainly onto state land, to make their living by subsistence agriculture. These squatters, being outside government control, became the commissariat and the 'popular base' for the insurgent movement. Similarly in Vietnam, large rural areas, even whole provinces, were dominated by the Viet Minh during the French war, and the administration was hardly restored under Ngo Dinh Diem before the Viet Cong challenged the newly independent government of South Vietnam.

The presence of this vital factor is not something that can be left to chance. All means are used to increase control in the rural areas, to cause general discontent and to discredit the government for the purpose of trying to break the links between the government and the people. It is essential for the communists to eliminate or neutralize potential opponents. There will be a spate of murders of village and hamlet officials, labour foremen and any other prominent citizens to whom the local population might look for leadership. The communists are normally careful, however, not to murder a popular person before he has been discredited. This discrediting can be done in several ways: perhaps by associating him with an unpopular aspect of government policy, or by accusing him of corruption, or, better still, of rape. There is no shortage of keen female party workers who are prepared to engineer a situation which will justify a charge of this nature. It does not have to be proved.

This policy of wholesale murder has a further purpose, which can only be described as selective terrorism designed to keep the local population completely cowed. It is a policy that is continued right through an insurgency in order to maintain ruthless control and to frighten any would-be supporters of the government. Communists are, however, careful not to undertake general terror against the population as a whole, except in rare instances for a specific purpose, such as the complete destruction of a village (Simpang Tiga in Malaya was an example). Where this has occurred—as in Malaya, when for a period buses were shot up and grenades thrown in cinemas, acts resulting in indiscriminate deaths amongst the local population—the error of these tactics was soon realized. If continued beyond a certain point, general terror may drive the people to support the government. Terror is more effective when selective. This allows the communists' behaviour towards the people as a whole to be good, and strict discipline is used to enforce it. Food and other supplies are paid for, particularly in disputed areas where the communists are still attempting to gain control, and where good behaviour may contrast favourably with government blunders.

When, during the insurgency period, retribution is coupled with terror, acts are committed whose brutality is hardly credible in a law-abiding western society. On one occasion in Quang Ngai Province, when the Viet Cong regained control over a village which had been in government hands for some time, they seized the headman and his family, disembowelled his wife in front of him, hacked off his children's arms and legs and then emasculated him. This method of dealing with 'traitors' is certainly an effective way of winning that 'popular support' which so endears insurgent movements to less well-informed critics of the local government and of those western governments which support it.

In the pre-insurgency circumstances of murder and terror, it is very likely that the normal processes of law and order will fail to cope with the situation; the police are unable to effect arrests for lack of witnesses, or the crime itself may not even be reported. If a case does reach court, the evidence may be inadequate to secure a conviction. I well remember a case in Perak when two Chinese terrorists murdered a Chinese mining foreman in his house at night. The police obtained statements from the family who witnessed the murder, as well as other evidence sufficient to arrest the two terrorists. When the case came before the magistrate's court, all the witnesses, although closely related to the murdered man, went back on the greater part of their statements. Even so, the evidence was sufficient for the case to be transferred to the High Court, since a capital offence was involved. When the case was called, all the prosecution witnesses refused to give evidence; their previous statements were of course inadmissible under the laws of evidence, and the accused were acquitted without their defence being called.

Fortunately the Resident Commissioner did not hesitate to use his powers under the Banishment Enactment to have the leading accused, who was an alien Chinese, re-arrested to show cause why he should not be deported to China. I was appointed to hold the enquiry, and was able to interview the witnesses in front of the accused, but not in public. Their lives had, of course, been threatened if they gave evidence in court, but they were prepared at the enquiry to confirm their original statements. Apart from recognizing the accused as the murderer, they had described him before his arrest as an unusually tall Hakka who spoke good Malay—a rare quality in a Chinese. He was also carrying a Gurkha kukri. The accused had been attached to a Gurkha battalion just after the re-occupation. But the most damning circumstantial evidence was that he had robbed the murdered man of $75 in five-dollar notes, and when arrested by the police shortly after in a cinema, he had on him exactly this sum less the price of his cinema ticket. He was duly deported to China, while his local-born accomplice went free.

The number of murders and abductions in Malaya, of which records are available, attributed to communist terrorism between October 1, 1945, and the end of June 1948, i.e.

before the Emergency began, was 298 (this excludes the interregnum before Malaya was re-occupied by British forces on the defeat of Japan). Of this figure, 107, over one-third, occurred in the first six months of 1948 just before the outbreak of the insurgency. The number of civilians murdered and abducted during the twelve years of the Emergency was 3,283 (compared with a total of 1,865 Security Forces killed in action). In Vietnam the figures are frightening, and it is estimated that well over 25,000 civilians were murdered or abducted between 1956 and 1965, excluding all battle casualties. The published figures for murders and abductions in 1960 and 1961 alone (the initial period of insurgency) show 6,130 murders and 6,213 abductions—a total of over 12,000.

Mao Tse-tung was right when he said that political power grows out of the barrel of a gun.

Chapter 3

Communist Insurgency

THE stage has been reached when the communists are ready for, but still not quite committed to, open insurgency. The main prong of their attack, subversion supported by selective terrorism, has reached a point at which they have to decide whether they can bring the government down by this means alone, or whether they will have to use the second prong of their attack, the 'armed struggle'. Insurgency is a measure both of the success and of the failure of subversion. The subversion has been successful enough for them to mount an insurgency, but not successful enough to win by subversion alone (as the Communist Party had probably hoped to do in Indonesia).

 There are other factors which may affect the start of an insurgency and its timing. In the case of Malaya, it is now known that instructions were received from Moscow through a communist conference held early in 1948 in Calcutta. The Malayan Communist Party was a well-placed pawn which Russia could not fail to use, and if necessary sacrifice, in the cold-war period of the Berlin air-lift and, later, Korea. In the case of Vietnam, direction from Hanoi and tacit support from China were probably equally decisive. From the communist point of view the outbreak of an insurgency is one of the more dangerous moments. If the insurgency is delayed, either the government may act first and pull in many key personnel who have been identified during the subversion stage, or the measures already taken by the government may be eroding the communist cause and the support amongst the population which it has engendered. For example, the economic and development programmes being carried out in Vietnam by President Diem in the late 1950s were beginning to make an impact which made the promises of the Viet Cong seem hollow in the light of unfavourable reports of conditions in North Vietnam. The threat of invidious comparisons cannot be tolerated either by the Ho Chi Minhs or Sukarnos of this world. On the other hand, if the outbreak is premature and inadequately planned, there is the risk that the initial actions may be dealt with by the government and that the whole movement will collapse, as in Brunei in 1962.

There was little risk either in Malaya or in Vietnam from the communist point of view of the insurgent movement being summarily put down in its opening stages. Neither government was prepared. In Malaya the government had failed to heed the signs and warnings, and the Police Force, which was to bear the brunt of the initial outbreak, had only just recovered to its pre-war strength of over 11,000. The Army units available to support the Police in Malaya were twelve, with a total strength of only about 10,000 men. In Vietnam the government was prepared for communist aggression on the Korean model, and not for insurgency within the country. In both countries the communists had little difficulty in recalling most of the men who had served in the resistance movements or the Viet Minh to their units, and arms, which had been cached away for this very purpose, were rapidly distributed. The jungle terrain provided a safe initial sanctuary.

Given an established base or sanctuary from which to work, the first aim of any insurgent movement must be to gain momentum by capturing more weapons, ammunition and explosives. Attacks will therefore be made on isolated police posts and stations, and even on military installations where security is lax. At the same time, these and other attacks, particularly on communications, will be designed to throw the government off balance, to cause panic in the population and to dislocate the economy. If these attacks in turn entice the government forces to go blundering around the countryside, so much the better.

If these are the initial aims, they are not of course the strategic aims of the guerilla phase of an insurgency, which must be clearly understood by those who wish to counter them. The political aim is to gain control over the population, starting in the rural areas, and to destroy the government's prestige and authority. The military aim is to neutralize the government's armed forces, and render them powerless to save the country. The general concept, as it is applied on the ground, is best summed up by a phrase of Mao Tse-tung's in which he states that the villages must be used to encircle the towns.

To carry out these aims there is a joint political and military organization, with the military always subordinate to the political. Support for the political aim of gaining control over the population by continued subversion and terror is always the primary task of the communist guerilla units. The organization is similar at every level in the communist hierarchy, whether region, province, district or village. It can best be shown in diagrammatic form using the district as an example:

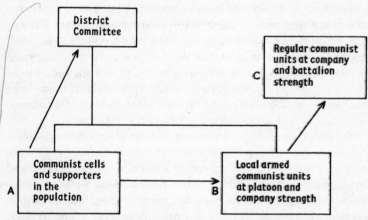

NOTE: C may or may not be stationed in every district, but is moved in to reinforce B for specific operations.

The communist political organization within the population at A is responsible, with the help of the armed military units at B and C outside the population, for expanding communist control over the population under the direction of the district committee. This contains both political and military members, and is normally located outside the population with one of the platoons at B. The political organization at A is also responsible for providing the district committee and the armed units at B and C with food, other supplies, recruits and intelligence. Thus traffic runs from A to B and thence to C as shown by the arrows. By expanding A and gaining control over larger areas and more population, the flow of supplies and recruits to the armed units steadily increases. In this way, such units can then be built up gradually from platoon to company and even battalion strength at the district level, and, based on a number of districts, the regular units can be built up from company to battalion and then to regimental strength.

A harassed government faced with this situation calls in its military commanders to deal with the insurgents. Quite naturally these commanders are inclined to regard the local and regular units at B and C as their main objective because militarily they present the only attractive targets. The net result is that large-scale military operations based on very meagre intelligence are mounted to seek out and destroy these units. Guerilla units are designed to cope with exactly this form of government reaction. To start with, they are seldom concentrated (except for an action on their own initiative), and are scattered over wide areas of jungle or other inaccessible terrain. Even if, as a matter of luck, the government forces make contact, the action is immediately broken off by the guerillas. In the very rare case when a unit is surrounded and caught in the open and suffers heavy casualties as a result, no permanent damage is inflicted. As soon as the government forces withdraw, the whole organization goes to work, and within a short period of perhaps two or three months the losses have been made good. For example, let us suppose that a regular company at C suffers fifty casualties; these are immediately replaced by promotions from the local units in the neighbourhood at B, and these in turn are reinforced by new recruits from the population, provided by the organization at A. This restoration of strength is not lost on the local population, and any confidence which such a victory might have restored in the government soon begins to wane.

The situation will develop into one in which the insurgents first gain control over the population and villages in the remoter valleys and on the fringes of jungle and swamp. Such areas are selected for reason of their inaccessibility to government forces, and are rendered more inaccessible by the cutting of any access roads and the blowing up of bridges. Road-cutting in Vietnam has been developed to a fine art, and it is not unusual to see from the air roads which have trenches cut across them to a depth of two or three feet every few yards. This work is carried out by the population under the control and supervision of a section of the political organization. Frequently, after one season of wet weather, the rain and floods pouring through these trenches eventually wash away the whole of the road-bed for several hundred yards. It becomes a major operation for the government forces even to re-enter such areas, let alone rebuild the road.

As soon as such areas are fully under insurgent control, and the political organization has extended its operations into the next stretch of populated territory, it becomes possible for the district platoon to move into the controlled area, where they can live in comparative safety and give the necessary support to the advancing political organization. Even the regular units can move down to the fringe of the populated area, and may even billet their forces on several outlying villages. Training camps for new recruits, however, are normally maintained still within the jungle areas, together with supplies and ammunition dumps and small armouries which are early established to make primitive weapons and to repair those which are damaged. If the necessary machinery can be purchased in a nearby town, these jungle armouries can even make heavier weapons such as mortars, as well as rifles and pistols. When it is well under way, a communist insurgent movement is normally organized on the lines of the diagram on the opposite page.

As the insurgent movement reaches into the more heavily populated rural areas, further opportunities occur for attacks on small isolated government posts, many of which will probably have been established in an attempt to provide protection for the population and as a barrier against the insurgent advance. In these areas there is more government patrol activity along such road networks as exist and along tracks between villages and posts. This provides the insurgent units with the opportunity for ambushes of small parties and for the mining of jeeps and trucks on the roads, as a result of

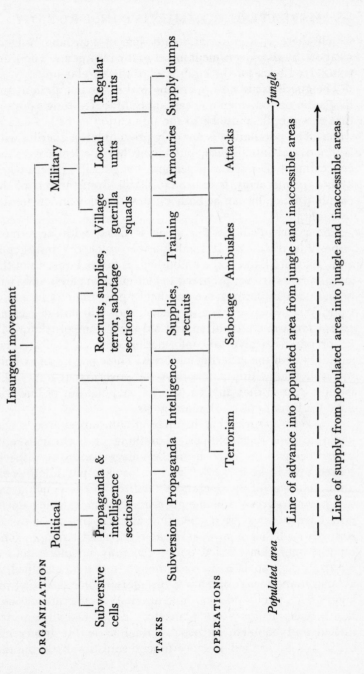

which there is a constant steady loss of new and modern weapons by the government forces to the insurgents. These are transferred back for the equipping of the regular units.

The guerillas are now operating within the population, and this is the period when one can apply Mao Tse-tung's dictum that the guerilla must be to the population as little fishes in water. The population is not only providing the guerilla with his food and intelligence, but giving him perfect cover and concealment. Dressed as a peasant, the guerilla, except when he is carrying arms, is indistinguishable from the rest of the people. In fact, he can be both a peasant by day and a guerilla by night.

The government at this stage is faced with an almost impossible dilemma. If small patrols enter the insurgents' area, they are liable to be ambushed. If forces larger than the guerilla units are yet prepared to face enter the area, they will be harassed by sniping fire and held up by mines and booby traps. When they arrive at a village, they will find it vacated except for women, children and old men, none of whom will be prepared to give any information or even to fraternize willingly with the government forces. These people know only too well that within a few days the government forces will withdraw, and that anyone who has stepped out of line will have his throat cut by the insurgents.

It is only natural that in these circumstances troops will begin to lose their temper. If nothing else, chickens and vegetables will be seized from the villages, and any suspects picked up will be ill treated and tortured to provide information. The size of the operations required to enter such areas will begin to grow, and the government forces, which up to now have perhaps been operating at company or battalion strength, will begin to operate at regimental strength. The type of operation carried out is generally no more than a sweep through such areas, even though it may be classified as a 'search-and-clear' operation or, more euphemistically, an 'aggressive search-and-clear' operation. As soon as any opposition is met, artillery and planes are called on, villages are shelled and bombed, and such casualties as the insurgents incur are multiplied in government statistics both by the bodies of innocent peasants killed and by a wishful but unreliable factor which dictates that bomb casualties are always counted in fives and tens. The communists are not slow to make propaganda capital out of all excesses committed by the government, with the result that most search-and-clear operations, by creating more communists than they kill, become in effect communist recruiting drives.*

* * *

At this point it is worth saying a few words about communist recruiting methods. Broadly, the recruits are of three types: the naturals, the converted and the deceived.*

The naturals consist of many elements, ranging from the idealist to the criminal. None of them see any future prospects for themselves in existing society. They do not want to follow in father's footsteps, they may have failed essential examinations, they may have suffered a period of unemployment, or they may have run foul of the law. (It is an interesting facet of an insurgency that normal crime figures, as opposed to terrorist crime, show a very marked drop.) For one such reason or another the naturals have a grudge, though they are influenced more by a desire to change the existing society than by the urge for revenge. They have great confidence in their own talents if only they held positions in which to demonstrate them. Communism, with its strength of purpose and discipline, with the chances of promotion in its monolithic structure, with its security of organization and its conspiratorial secrecy, with its belief in inevitable victory and its sense of political power, offers them their opportunity.

The converted include those who join because of government excesses or abuses of power. Members of their family may have been killed by government operations, or imprisoned or tortured for aiding the insurgents. They also include those

---

* For a first-class study of the influences and pressures which induced young Chinese to join the Malayan Communist Party and subsequently to surrender, the reader is recommended to read *Guerrilla Communism in Malaya: Its Social and Political Meaning* by Lucian W. Pye (Princeton University Press, 1956).

who are persuaded to join the insurgent ranks because they have close friends in them. Finally, if things are going well for the insurgents, there are those who, out of self-interest, do not want to leave it too late to climb on the band-wagon and join the winning side. This category includes members of the government forces who are captured or subverted. (This was a very large element in the communist victory in China, when complete Nationalist battalions changed sides.)

The deceived category include some of the above. In any communist appeal there is always a degree of deception which simple minds are unable to detect. It is very easy to persuade young people to hold discussions, which gradually become more politically inclined, to carry out social welfare work with a political bias and to collect subscriptions for it. It remains only to develop a situation in which they come up against authority, whether parental, educational or governmental. When authority reacts, it is then simple to turn fear of punishment or even arrest to the communist advantage. If the path from the discussion group to a jungle training camp is a gentle slope, it can be made more slippery by the prospect of excitement and action. There are not many boys who, when offered a rifle and told to fire at all passing aircraft, could possibly resist the temptation.

But the two main elements in the category of the deceived are those who earlier joined the insurgent ranks for legitimate reasons (for example, the resistance movement) and subsequently found themselves committed to the communist cause, and youths abducted from their villages, frequently in groups of ten or twenty. Such a group is then escorted to a jungle camp for training and indoctrination. At the right moment it is taken out on a final exercise armed with primitive weapons, but led by a few well-armed hard-core instructors. The group descends on an undefended village or ambushes a civilian vehicle. The headman or other innocent civilians are murdered, and the group, with blood on its hands, is made to feel irrevocably committed to the communist cause.

As in any army, therefore, there are the volunteers and the conscripts. The system produces its heroes and, when times are hard, its traitors. At least it should be recognized that, by reason of their sources of recruitment, guerillas are not a race apart and ten foot tall. They can be just as frightened as you or I.

*   *   *

So the guerilla phase goes on, perhaps for several years. The insurgents' control in the populated areas is slowly but steadily expanding. These areas of expansion are carefully selected. They may have been areas with a long history of communist penetration, dating from the resistance period, in which the authority of any subsequent post-war government has been weak. They are also likely to be areas along the boundary lines between government administrative regions or provinces in which there is a lack of co-ordination on the part of the government. Guerilla units can often find sanctuary merely by crossing such boundaries from one government operational area to another. They will normally be the least accessible areas, and in themselves may pose no great threat to the general security and economy of the country. Certain such areas will also be important to the guerillas as the passage-ways between their main jungle base areas that allow recruits and supplies to be more easily deployed.

There is a very clear distinction between the jungle bases and what the communist insurgents call their 'popular' bases. The jungle bases are areas where, without much risk of interference, guerilla units can obtain rest and sanctuary, where ammunition, food and other supplies can be stored in numerous caches, and where recruits can be trained and tactical headquarters established. There is nothing permanent about any of this. Huts and clearings in the jungle can be made in two or three days, and even if a superior government force succeeds in finding and destroying some of them, they can be rapidly re-established nearby, in the same jungle base area. The 'popular' bases, by contrast, are the villages under insurgent control from which most of the supplies and recruits are obtained in the first place. There is an analogy here with a fleet at sea, which can use some tropical island and lagoon as its ocean (jungle) base, but which must finally depend on its home ports (popular bases) as the source of its supplies and reinforcements. If an ocean base is put out of action, no permanent damage is done to the fleet's operational capabilities. But if the home ports are destroyed, the operating endurance of the fleet is immediately limited.

Throughout the whole guerilla phase the political organization is continuing to expand its control in the populated areas and is maintaining its links with the cells previously established in the towns and the nation's capital. These cells have two main functions besides that of expanding their subversive network. The first is to maintain a continual propaganda barrage, supported by terrorist acts, including the assassination of prominent citizens who might rally elements in the population to the government cause. A good example of this was the murder of Dr Ong Chong Kheng of Penang, who was falsely summoned one night to a sick-bed, only to be murdered by two young terrorists on his arrival. The second function is to keep the guerillas supplied with intelligence of government activities and plans, and also with special articles of supply, such as radio and printing equipment, armourers' tools and medicines which are not obtainable from village sources. As the government authority in the rural areas is eroded, so the penetration of the towns is stepped up, and every effort is made to infiltrate government ministries and the security forces. This does not mean that communist agents are inserted, unless it has already been done many years before, but that pressure can be brought to bear on individuals, either by blackmail or by appealing to their self-interest, to support the communist cause or at least to do nothing to hinder it. Promises of safety for their families and of reasonable employment in the event of a communist victory begin to carry weight with the weak-hearted.

A loss of morale in the civilian population is likely to occur quicker than in the government forces, where there is greater discipline. This particularly applies to the regular troops, who, though they may become discouraged and less aggressive, will still remain capable of putting up a stiff fight if attacked or if attacking under favourable conditions. The many abortive operations, however, in which they will have taken part begin to take their toll, and the confidence of the troops in those directing the war effort is not improved by information blurbs issued by the government claiming victories which in many instances the troops themselves know to be false.

A more dangerous loss of morale will occur in the police and other local territorial forces of a para-military nature which will have borne the brunt of the insurgents' advance into the populated areas. They will have suffered heavy casualties and a loss of weapons on an increasingly large scale; recruiting difficulties will have caused units to be greatly under strength; officer material will almost certainly be poor and inexperienced. And, to add to this, the insurgents will not have neglected the use of terrorist tactics to reduce morale in these units still further. A typical example of this was the Viet Cong attack on the Civil Guard post at Cai Be in July 1964, which was defended by part of a Civil Guard company, while the remainder were out on patrol duties. The post housed the families of the company. Forty women and children were killed, including the wife and all five young children of the lieutenant commanding the company. The civilians in the immediately adjacent district town were not affected, except by overthrows, but the viciousness of the attack was not lost on them. They could not have been more silent and sullen on the following day.

As government units fall below strength, possibly by as much as 50 per cent in some of the para-military forces in bad areas, exactly the opposite is taking place with regard to guerilla units. Companies that were previously seventy strong are one hundred and fifty strong; regular battalions which were two hundred strong increase to five hundred. The only real limiting factor is the supply of weapons, but these are now being lost by the government in ever-increasing numbers, particularly if they have been indiscriminately distributed in the first place. The figures of weapon gains and losses are, indeed, one of the most reliable guides to the course of the war. It may be of interest to give some figures of weapon gains and losses in Malaya and Vietnam. A point to remember is that insurgent losses are generally of older and more obsolete weapons, whereas the government losses are of new and modern weapons. The Malayan figures (annual) were as follows:

Period	Lost	Recovered
1948 (6 months)	100	497
1949	214	930
Critical period		
1950	551	650
1951	770	927
1952	487	1,170
1953	159	1,139
Expansion of Home Guard		
1954	203	799
1955	207	625
1956	88	444
1957	43	389
Mass surrenders		
1958	7	754
1959	—	122
1960	—	18
TOTALS	2,829	8,464

The following are the figures for Vietnam (quarterly) from August 1962 to the end of 1964:

Period	Lost	Recovered
Strategic hamlet period		
September 1962 (2 months) . .	843	902
December 1962	1,172	1,451
March 1963	1,192	1,319
Buddhist controversy		
June 1963	1,862	1,265
September 1963	2,598	1,086
Collapse of strategic hamlets and fall of President Diem		
December 1963	2,833	1,253
Successive changes of government and larger-scale guerilla actions		
March 1964	2,366	1,470
June 1964	2,222	977
September 1964	4,703	1,360
December 1964	4,746	1,569
TOTALS	24,537	12,652

Whereas in Malaya the losses and recoveries were in an increasing and then a decreasing curve, with the advantage always to the government, in Vietnam the losses showed a mounting trend, while the recoveries were fairly constant between 1,000 and 1,500.

To return to insurgent strengths, it often comes as a surprise to people that regular guerilla units are able to increase their strength in spite of the fact that they have been suffering quite heavy casualties in continuous operations over perhaps several years. The answer is fairly simple: the size of their forces as compared with the population under their control is relatively very low. For example, in 1964 the Viet Cong territorial and regular units, excluding village guerillas, were estimated to number about 35,000 and to have suffered casualties between 15,000 and 20,000 annually over the previous two years. The base of the population under their control, however, was nearly five million people by the end of 1964. To maintain units at this strength, and even to increase them, is no problem when it is realized that in the United Kingdom in the Second World War, with all the simultaneous industrial output required, the country was able to raise for the Army alone (excluding Navy and Air Force) the equivalent of about one division to every million of the population.

It is at this point that the guerilla phase of the war begins to achieve both its military and its political aims. Militarily, the government forces, as the villages begin to encircle the towns, are forced back in defence of the country's main infrastructure. More and more are deployed to garrison district and provincial towns and to defend vital installations and communications, including bridges, power lines, oil depots and airfields. A few calculated guerilla attacks, such as that on Bien Hoa airfield near Saigon on November 1, 1964, accelerate this process. Static defence in penny packets becomes the order of the day, providing still more comparatively easy targets for a well-planned guerilla night attack, and neutralizing any offensive capacity left in the armed forces. In many district and provincial towns, government forces will be unable to go outside the perimeter, and there may even be a local gentlemen's agreement that, if they do not, they will not be attacked.

Besides, the insurgents do not yet want to capture and hold such towns. They are still a useful source of supply while in government hands, and guerillas do not want to be encumbered with the administrative and defence problems involved. Militarily the guerilla strategy of using the villages to encircle the towns is achieving its purpose of rendering an as yet undefeated army powerless to save the country.

The guerilla phase will also have had its political effects. Trade will be virtually at a standstill, and prices of local produce will begin to rise, causing yet more discontent in the towns. Government revenue will be falling, and the value of money steadily depreciating. There will be a growing loss of confidence in the government, if this has not already occurred, as in Vietnam, where, in November 1963, two allied but completely conflicting forces, reinforced by the emotions of American liberalism, overthrew the government and killed President Diem. These two conflicting forces were those who still wanted to win the war and thought they could run it better, and those who wanted to overthrow a dedicated but authoritarian anti-communist government in order to seek a peaceful and neutralist solution. The Viet Cong could not have engineered it better.

As the guerilla phase reaches its climax, another critical period for the insurgents develops. They are faced with three methods of achieving final political victory. The first is to seek a military victory by the classical solution, laid down by Mao Tse-tung, of changing from guerilla warfare to a war of movement. With the government forces stretched throughout the country in a defensive role, the insurgent forces are able to occupy completely vast populated rural areas and to move their forces throughout them at will. They can at this stage concentrate at divisional strength and may even acquire heavy weapons, including artillery, either by capture or by outside supply. To start a war of movement, particularly if some of the country through which units must operate is fairly open, is a risky procedure when the government still has a superiority of forces, the striking power of an air force and the ability to move troops quickly by air. One major defeat for the insurgents in a large-scale set-piece battle might give the government its opportunity to stage a successful comeback. A real war of movement was waged in China, where the size of the country and of the forces involved made such a course necessary. In the Indo-China war, however, a premature attempt in the Red River Delta in 1950-51 to introduce a war of movement resulted in heavy Viet Minh losses. It was not repeated except in the special single case of Dien Bien Phu, when the French tactically placed themselves in such an unfavourable position that a major battle, involving guerilla forces more than 20,000 strong, was made worth the risk for the political results which it would achieve. So far as small countries in Asia or elsewhere are concerned, it is unfortunately more likely than not that a war of movement would be unnecessary to achieve the final political victory, though it remains available if all other means fail.

The second method is simpler and, from all points of view, more satisfactory. It is to maintain the military pressure by guerilla action, without seeking major battles such as Dien Bien Phu to achieve the final victory, and at the same time to encourage all groups within the population that have been penetrated to bring pressure to bear on a demoralized government, until the point is reached at which certain members of the government can be induced to negotiate a cease-fire and to accept a neutralist solution as a means of ending the war. This was the situation which seemed to be developing in Vietnam at the beginning of 1965. At this point, after constant changes of government and two abortive *coups d'état*, there was every prospect that a government might be formed containing elements prepared to negotiate a cease-fire, after which an ostensibly neutralist coalition government with the National Liberation Front would have been formed. Having invited the American Military Assistance Command to leave, and given it plenty of time and all facilities to do so, the new government would then have spent the necessary time in establishing full control before proposing reunification with North Vietnam as the final solution. This, or something very like it, would have provided a comparatively smooth and tidy means of effecting a communist take-over.

The third method is a development of the second when the

government cannot be induced to negotiate a cease-fire. The military pressure, still by guerilla action, will be intensified, with the aim of further demoralizing the government forces and of forcing increasing numbers of the rural community to seek refuge in the towns, thereby raising for the government all the additional problems connected with refugees on a large scale. With effective government already badly eroded, and vocal and critical groups well penetrated, it only requires a hotting up of terrorist incidents in the towns to get the pot nicely boiling. Such incidents will be ostensibly directed against those responsible for continuing the war, especially foreign supporters of the government, but will be really intended to hurt the civil population.

Two good examples of this form of terrorism were the blowing up in 1965 of the American Embassy in Saigon and of the My Canh floating restaurant. The ostensible target was Americans, but the real intention was to kill and maim as many Vietnamese as possible. Twelve Americans were killed in these outrages, but over forty Vietnamese died as well. The ultimate aim of this form of terrorism, with all the other factors present in such a situation, is to engineer what is called a popular mass uprising against the government and its foreign supporters. If this gets out of control, it will result in chaos and the complete collapse of organized government. It is a rough, untidy but effective way of achieving the final victory and a communist take-over.

*   *   *

This survey of an insurgency would not be complete without considering the case when a communist insurgent movement is defeated in the guerilla phase, as in Malaya. In 1948, when the Emergency broke out, the insurgent forces were rapidly built up to a strength of about 5,000 in recognizable units. This corresponds almost exactly with the situation which developed in Vietnam in about the middle of 1960. In Malaya by 1951 it was estimated that the communist guerilla units had a total strength of over 10,000, and that they were actively supported by nearly 50,000 persons in the population.

Insurgency put down by gov. in Malaya 1954
Mopping up operations took place after this
COMMUNIST INSURGENCY   45

As already stated, the main impact of government measures occurred during the period when Sir Gerald Templer was High Commissioner, from 1952 to 1954, and it was during this period that the communists' organization and military strength were broken, so that by the end of 1954 their eventual military defeat became apparent. Their strength was declining rapidly; they were losing arms at a higher rate than the government, and their subversive political organization was being uprooted. Politically, this enabled the British to set the date for independence in 1957 and to inaugurate countrywide elections for a Malayan government, which was established in 1955 with Tunku Abdul Rahman as Chief Minister.

When facing defeat both militarily and politically, there is only one gambit for a Communist Party to play, and that is to take the famous 'one step backward', except that in this case it had to be considerably more than one step. With a new Malayan government in the saddle, pledged in its election platform to offer an amnesty to end war, the Communist Party accordingly put out peace feelers. The military pressure was temporarily taken off, and arrangements were made for peace talks to be held at Baling near the Malayan-Thai frontier. Tunku Abdul Rahman led the government delegation, and Chin Peng represented the Malayan Communist Party. The latter argued hard for reasonable terms, but in the end offered to lay down arms on the one condition that, with independence, the Malayan Communist Party would be recognized as a legal political party and allowed to take part in future elections and the political life of the country. The Tunku was too old a hand to buy that one. He offered instead an amnesty under which all persons, if they laid down their arms, would be given fair treatment, being subsequently allowed, if they showed their good intentions, to become citizens of the country; if they did not, they would be shipped back to China. This was refused by the Malayan Communist Party, and the mopping-up period of the Emergency began.

The insurgent aim during this mopping-up period was twofold. First, the communists obviously wanted to salvage and keep in being as many of their guerilla units as possible, and there was a steady withdrawal of small remnants from all

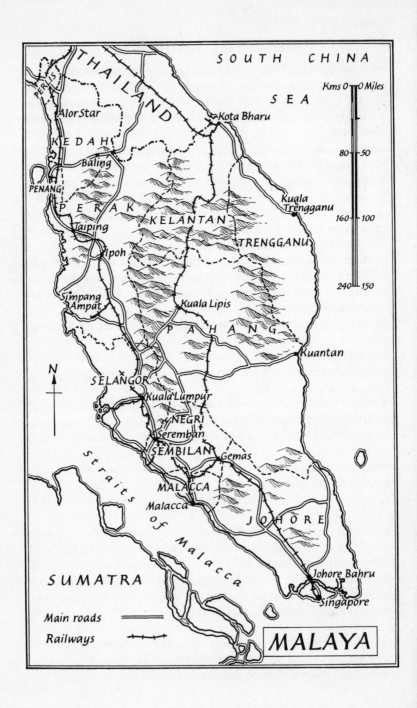

SOUTH CHINA
SEA

THAILAND

PERLIS

Alor Star

KEDAH

Baling

PENANG

PERAK

Taiping

Ipoh

Simpang
Ampat

Kota Bharu

KELANTAN

Kuala
Trengganu

TRENGGANU

Kuala Lipis

PAHANG

Kuantan

Kms 0   0 Miles

80 — 50

160 — 100

240 — 150

N

SELANGOR

Kuala Lumpur

NEGRI

Seremban

SEMBILAN

Gemas

MALACCA

Malacca

JOHORE

Straits of Malacca

SUMATRA

Johore Bahru

Singapore

Main roads

Railways

MALAYA

over North Malaya towards the mountain jungles on the Thai frontier. Only about 500 succeeded in escaping in this way and the remainder, numbering approximately 2,500, were eliminated or surrendered in the five years 1955-60. The communists second and main aim was to reform their subversive political organization within the population, and in this, thanks to a highly developed police intelligence service, they had only a limited success, rather more in Singapore than in Malaya, in penetrating Chinese schools, Nanyang University and some left-wing political parties. With an efficient and respected Police Force, and the population protected and co-operative, terrorism almost ceased to be an effective weapon in support of subversion. This subversion, however, was reinforced by a subtle propaganda drive from communist China directed at the young Chinese and appealing to them in terms of Chinese nationalism, not communism.

The whole intention of the Malayan Communist Party was, of course, to await a future favourable opportunity for renewing the struggle. That opportunity later presented itself in the current 'confrontation' between Indonesia and Malaysia. This policy was adopted by Sukarno under pressure from the Communist Party of Indonesia, which had taken over from the Malayan Communist Party (mainly Chinese) the direction of the struggle. The lesson to be learnt is that even if an armed insurgency is defeated, the political and subversive struggle will go on and can still win, as in Algeria.

*   *   *

It is interesting to compare the respective strengths of the insurgents and government forces as between Malaya and Vietnam. As already stated, in both countries the initial strengths of the insurgents' forces were approximately 4,000-5,000, which built up in Malaya to a maximum of 10,000 and then steadily declined. In Vietnam, between 1960 and the beginning of 1965, the strength was built up to an estimated 35,000-40,000. The number of active positive supporters outside these guerilla units cannot be accurately given, but it was roughly estimated in Malaya at the height of the

Emergency at about 50,000, and in Vietnam at about 100,000.

At the beginning of the Emergency in Malaya, the immediate strength of the government forces was about 21,000 (a ratio of roughly five to one over the armed communist terrorists excluding supporters). This ratio was steadily improved, mainly by the expansion of the Police Force, until in the crucial period in the early 1950s the ratio was about twelve to one. Thereafter, as the Home Guard was expanded and the terrorist strength declined, the ratio increased to over twenty-five to one and continued steadily upwards. The part-time Home Guard eventually reached a figure of 250,000, of which less than 50,000 were ever on duty and armed at any one time. By the time these numbers were reached, the strengths of both the Police Force and the Armed Forces were being allowed to decline from their respective maximums of about 60,000 and 30,000. But, with the insurgent strength declining, the ratio in favour of the government was overwhelming.

In Vietnam the trend has been almost exactly the reverse. Initially, the ratio in favour of the government was over fifty to one. By 1963, in spite of some expansion of the government forces and the formation of a full-time hamlet militia, the ratio had fallen to under twenty-five to one as a result of the armed Viet Cong units having increased their strength to nearly 25,000. Subsequently, with the Viet Cong steadily increasing to nearly 40,000 and the government strength declining, as a result of the losses suffered by the para-military forces and especially the hamlet militia, the favourable ratio dropped still further, so that by the beginning of 1965 it was about ten to one. The decline continued rapidly until the arrival of American combat troops. It remains to be seen whether it can be halted.

There are many who say that a government cannot win an insurgency unless it has a favourable strength ratio of at least ten to one over the insurgent, and who thereby imply that the government forces must be expanded, or outside forces introduced, until that ratio is achieved. This is nonsense and rates as one of the myths of counter-insurgency. It is rather like saying that you can win the ball-game by altering the scoreboard. The rise, or fall, in the ratio is one of the indicators of how the war is going. Obviously a government can expand its forces, but only within limits. There are many factors in this which have to be taken into account (as will appear later), including such considerations as the need to involve large numbers of people on the side of the government. The real crux is whether, while expanding, the government is at the same time taking other action to ensure that the insurgent rate of expansion is correspondingly slower so that the favourable ratio is steadily improved. It is clearly better to have a favourable ratio of five to one which is improving, rather than a ratio of fifteen to one which is declining. The magic figure of ten to one, therefore, is not a prerequisite but an indicator. If it is reached on an improving trend (or an initial higher ratio is maintained), the government is on the way to victory, but if it is reached on a declining trend, then the fault lies elsewhere and will not be corrected by raising yet more forces.

What needs to be recognized is that, in spite of ready acceptance of their grandiloquent and misleading titles, a communist armed insurgency is not a 'People's Revolutionary War'. It will be seen from the figures already given that the insurgents' strengths, including active supporters, in both Malaya and Vietnam (until the end of 1964) were at no stage any more than one per cent of the population, and initially a great deal less than that. This does not qualify an insurgency as a 'People's Revolutionary War', but only as a revolutionary form of warfare designed to enable a very small ruthless minority to gain control over the people.

While Malayan insurgents were decreasing the Viet insurgents were gaining in number and strength

Chapter 4

Basic Principles of Counter-Insurgency

I HAVE endeavoured in the first three chapters to give a general idea of some of the problems which face a government during the three main phases of an insurgency. Two obvious points emerge from this. The first is that any sensible government should attempt to defeat an insurgent movement during the subversive build-up phase before it enters the guerilla phase, and if that is not possible owing to circumstances perhaps outside the government's control, then the movement must be defeated as early as possible during the guerilla phase. Unfortunately, during the build-up phase, the signs are not always recognized, and the existence of a subversive movement may even be ignored or denied for short-sighted political reasons. It is not easy for a government to alert its people to the danger. If restrictive measures are successfully taken, there will be little evidence of subversion, and the government runs the risk of being accused of repression. If, on the other hand, subversion leads to insurgency, there will then be plenty of evidence, but the government has a war on its hands.

The second point is that anyone having any responsibility for dealing with an insurgent movement must know his enemy and what that enemy is attempting to do at all stages. This does not mean that those responsible should be solely concerned with countering the enemy's moves. I dislike for this reason the very term 'counter-insurgency'. It implies that the insurgents have the initiative, and that it is the government's role merely to react and counter that initiative.

Accepting, therefore, that prevention is better than cure, and that the government must be positive in its approach, I suggest that there are five basic principles which must be followed and within which all government measures must fall.

First principle. The government must have a clear political aim: to establish and maintain a free, independent and united country which is politically and economically stable and viable.

It may be contended that this is rather too broad, if desirable, an aim; but in newly independent or underdeveloped territories it is essential to recognize that an insurgent movement is only one of the problems with which such governments are faced. The insurgency may demand priority, but it cannot be treated in isolation. For example, in most Asian territories there is an explosive population problem, with an annual growth rate of over 3 per cent. The development of the country to meet this problem can be just as vital as the defeat of the insurgent movement. It would be futile to succeed in defeating the insurgency, especially by military means alone during its guerilla phase, if the end result is a country which is not politically and economically viable, and which might therefore fall to the communists at any moment in the future, perhaps without a shot being fired.

An insurgent movement is a war for the people. It stands to reason that government measures must be directed to restoring government authority and law and order throughout the country, so that control over the population can be regained and its support won. This cannot be done unless a high priority is given to the administrative structure of government itself, to its institutions and to the training of its personnel. Without a reasonably efficient government machine, no programmes or projects, in the context of counter-insurgency, will produce the desired results.

I have already stressed the great advantage which the communists derive from weaknesses in the government and seeds of conflict within the community—what they term the 'contradictions'. By nibbling away and maintaining pressure, they can use these as a powerful lever for toppling the government. Corruption, for example, was an important factor in the downfall of Nationalist China. The correction of these weaknesses is as much a part of counter-insurgency as any military operation. In fact, it is far more important because unless the cracks in the government structure are mended, military operations and emergency measures, apart from being ineffectual, may themselves widen the cracks and be turned to the enemy's advantage.

Unless the long-term aim is constantly borne in mind, there will be a tendency to adopt short-term *ad hoc* measures merely as reactions to insurgent initiative or with the limited aim of attempting to defeat the insurgents militarily in the guerilla phase. A good example in Vietnam was the proliferation of provinces; these were increased from thirty-seven in 1956 to forty-five in 1964. The new provinces were created solely for military and security reasons as sector commands, and completely lacked the administrative backing necessary to enable them to function as provinces. In circumstances in which there is a shortage of trained staff but in which modern means of communication are available, the fewer the centres of authority outside the capital, the easier it is for the central government ministries to control and supervise the execution of policy. In South Vietnam, thirty provinces would have been enough and twenty-five better.

Another example was the establishment of a multitude of forces to meet special counter-insurgency tasks, resulting in an indiscriminate issue of arms. When asked towards the end of 1962 what was the total distribution of American weapons to the Vietnamese, an American general informed me that it was equivalent to fifty-one divisions. When I then asked what were the plans for recovering these after victory, he shrewdly replied: 'That is a problem which will worry neither you nor me!'

Second principle. The government must function in accordance with law.

There is a very strong temptation in dealing both with terrorism and with guerilla actions for government forces to act outside the law, the excuses being that the processes of law are too cumbersome, that the normal safeguards in the law for the individual are not designed for an insurgency and that a terrorist deserves to be treated as an outlaw anyway. Not only is this morally wrong, but, over a period, it will create more practical difficulties for a government than it solves. A government which does not act in accordance with the law forfeits the right to be called a government and cannot then expect its people to obey the law. Functioning in accordance with the law is a very small price to pay in return for the advantage of being the government.

Action in accordance with the law was a vital factor during the Huk insurgency in the Philippines, where Magsaysay made a reality of the constitution, and in Malaya, where the civil courts functioned normally throughout the Emergency. Statute law can be modified by emergency law, and laws of procedure and evidence can be simplified. There is nothing to prevent a government enacting very tough laws to cope with the situation, but the golden rule should be that each new law must be effective and must be fairly applied. It is no good enacting laws which cannot be enforced, thereby bringing the government into disrepute, or which fall unfairly on particular groups in the population.

Some very tough laws were enacted in Malaya. One enabled the government to seize and deport all Chinese found in a declared bad area. Another allowed the government to impose a collective fine on all the inhabitants of an area where the people were unco-operative. Both these laws were dropped after being used only two or three times because they were unfair on innocent members of the population. On the other hand, laws imposing strict curfews, a mandatory death penalty for carrying arms, life imprisonment for providing supplies or other support to terrorists, restricted residence or detention for suspected terrorist supporters and so on were introduced and effectively used. The main point about them was that they were seen by the population to be effective and were applied equally to all. The population knew what the law was, and because the government itself functioned in accordance with law and could be held responsible in the courts for its actions, the population could be required to fulfil its own obligation to obey the laws.

Detention is perhaps one of the most controversial powers which a government may exercise. If the power to arrest and detain is clearly laid down within certain limits and the individual is given a full opportunity to appear, represented by counsel, before a tribunal presided over by a judge which advises the government whether or not the case against the detainee is adequate, then there are sufficient safeguards to prevent the power being used for purely arbitrary arrests. It should be recognized that it is the aim of detention to prevent suspected persons from carrying out hostile acts. It is a power that most western governments have taken in time of war, and it cannot be denied to governments which face a national emergency caused by terrorism and insurgency.

As a corollary of preventive detention, it should be the firm policy of the government to bring all persons who have committed an actual offence to public trial. This has the great advantage not only of showing that justice is being done, but of spotlighting the brutality of terrorist crimes and the whole nature of the insurgent conspiracy, including any direction and assistance received from outside the country. The evidence is there for all to hear, and it automatically receives the fullest publicity at home and abroad. If the due processes of the law are followed, no justifying statements by the government are required. Trials in camera, martial law and military tribunals can never be satisfactorily justified. They are in themselves a tacit admission that responsible government has broken down. In the long term, adherence to the law is a great advantage to the government. It helps to make all officers and civilian officials responsible and accountable for their actions. It puts torture and the shooting of captured terrorists in their proper place: however great the provocation, both are crimes and the latter is murder. It puts the government in a position in which it is represented as a protector of those who are innocent, and it puts the terrorists in the position of criminals. This creates the proper psychological attitude in the country as a whole, with the government as the 'cops' and the terrorists as the 'robbers'.

If the government does not adhere to the law, then it loses respect and fails to fulfil its contractual obligation to the people as a government. This leads to the situation in which officers and officials cease to be responsible for their actions, with the result that, instead of an insurgency, there is to all intents and purposes a civil war within the country in which neither side can claim to be the government. In such circumstances there is so little difference between the two sides that the people have no reason for choosing to support the government.

I remember saying to General Khanh, then Prime Minister in Vietnam, that when I heard of a case of a peasant sueing the government for a buffalo killed by the army during operations and being paid compensation, we would be winning the war. A police constable stopping a general's car and summoning him for a traffic offence would have been too much to hope for.

Third principle. The government must have an overall plan.

This plan must cover not just the security measures and military operations. It must include all political, social, economic, administrative, police and other measures which have a bearing on the insurgency. Above all it must clearly define roles and responsibilities to avoid duplication of effort and to ensure that there are no gaps in the government's field of action.

It is essential, too, that there should be a proper balance between the military and the civil effort, with complete co-ordination in all fields. Otherwise a situation will arise in which military operations produce no lasting results because they are unsupported by civil follow-up action. Similarly, civilian measures, particularly in areas disputed with the insurgents, are a waste of time and money if they are unsupported by military operations to provide the necessary protection.

Because a government's resources, notably in trained man-power, are limited, the plan must also lay down priorities both in the measures to be taken and in the areas to be dealt with first. If the insurgency is country-wide, it is impossible to tackle it offensively in every area. It must be accepted that in certain areas only a holding operation can be conducted.

The plan must be positive, forcing the insurgents to react to government measures, but flexible enough to take advantage of success. Only in this way can the initiative be held. If there is no plan or if the plan is not followed consistently, then gradually but perceptibly the government will find itself in the position of merely reacting to insurgent initiative. From this position it is not easy to recover.

Fourth principle. The government must give priority to defeating the political subversion, not the guerillas.

This is obviously the case in the build-up phase before the insurgency has started, but it holds equally good during the insurgency. Unless the communist subversive political organization in the towns and villages is broken and eliminated, the insurgent guerilla units will not be defeated. If the guerillas can be isolated from the population, i.e. the 'little fishes' removed from 'the water', then their eventual destruction becomes automatic.

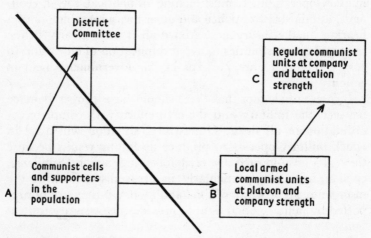

NOTE: C may or may not be stationed in every district, but is moved in to reinforce B for specific operations.

This can be made clear by repeating the earlier diagram, again at district level, and drawing through it a heavy line to indicate where all government attention should be focussed. If the subversive political organization at A can be eliminated, then the guerilla units at B and C, being short of supplies, recruits and intelligence, will be steadily reduced by a process of attrition until their members are either killed or surrender.

In the process of eliminating the political organization, the attention of the intelligence organization should also be directed to identifying, and eliminating if possible, all members of the insurgent organization who for one reason or another have to cross this heavy line between the insurgent units and the population. This should then be followed up by civilian measures and military operations designed to break the contact between the guerilla units and the subversive political organization. As this process develops, the guerilla units will themselves be forced to cross the line in an attempt to make contact with, and support, their political organization and to secure their sources of supply. The area of the heavy line is turned into a sort of barrier, and will become the killing ground because the guerillas will be forced to fight the government where it is ready for them and at its greatest strength. If the guerilla units fail to pierce the barrier and to regain contact with the subversive political organization and with the population on which they depend for support, they will be forced to retire to the jungles and swamps and to disperse into smaller and smaller units in order to maintain their day-to-day existence. The mopping-up period can then begin.

Fifth principle. In the guerilla phase of an insurgency, a government must secure its base areas first.

This principle should to a large extent be reversed in the build-up phase, before the open insurgency starts, when considerable attention should be paid to security and economic measures in the remoter rural areas. If, however, such preventive action fails, priority in respect of security measures should be given to the more highly developed areas of the country. These contain the greatest number of the population and are more vital to the government from the point of view of its communications and the economy of the country. This may mean accepting that the insurgent movement gains control over certain remoter areas and that there will be a degree of infiltration across inaccessible borders (which cannot be prevented anyway at this stage). Such infiltration will initially be limited in any case by the absorptive capacity of the areas under insurgent control. But if the area under the insurgents' control expands and the base of their support broadens, the absorptive capacity will increase. It must therefore be one of the government's aims to limit that capacity by securing its own base areas and working methodically outwards from them.

There is a second advantage in this approach: the more

But what if cities can't be secured

highly developed areas of the country are easier to secure and control, and the government will therefore start the campaign with some successes. This instils confidence, which is quite the most important ingredient for further success. A thoroughly methodical approach to the problem, which may appear rather slow, encourages a steam-roller outlook which provides the people with faith in ultimate victory. By preparing for a long haul, the government may achieve victory quicker than expected. By seeking quick military victories in insurgent controlled areas, it will certainly get a long haul for which neither it nor the people may be prepared.

*   *   *

Partly as a result of a sound administrative structure and a strong independent judiciary, which made the second principle sacred, these principles gradually emerged in Malaya by a process of trial and error rather than conscious decision. They were helped by an imaginative approach to the political problem and by a strictly methodical approach to the practical problems. South Vietnam lacked the necessary administrative structure and judicial system and had little time in which to develop them. Moreover, after independence, it was saddled with a major policy decision which either offended, or caused an inevitable breach of, all the principles. This was the creation of a large conventional army.

This decision stemmed from the lessons of Korea, not those of the Philippines and Malaya, and resulted from a wrong assessment of the threat, which at that time was considered to be direct aggression by the armed forces of communist North Vietnam. A large conventional South Vietnamese army, numbering eventually over 200,000, was established as a deterrent to this threat.

The inevitable effect of creating such a large army was that political power in the country rested entirely with control of the army. President Diem was forced to devote much of his time and energy to manipulating the army commands in order to retain control and maintain his position. All efforts to encourage him to broaden the base of his government and attract more popular support were meaningless in a situation in which the reality of political power lay not with the people but with the army. That he lasted for nine years through several attempted coups was a great tribute both to his own political sagacity and to that of his brother Ngo Dinh Nhu. His successors after the *coup d'état* of November 1, 1963, were not so adroit. One of the illuminating remarks which President Diem made in 1962 was that any successor, if he wished to maintain an effective government, would have to be twice as repressive as he himself had been. He also said to me more than a year before the final coup: 'Aprés moi le déluge!' How right he was.

In this respect, the fact that the army was conventionally organized with corps and divisional commands created a warlord outlook in the senior commanders and fired their ambitions. In a long dissertation one afternoon on the ancient history and administration of Vietnam, President Diem told me that successful generals were always retired. He had recourse to this step himself on occasion, but few of the present generals made their mark as senior commanders, and all owed what little success they had to the presence and support of President Diem behind them. On their own they lacked the experience or ability to command much more than a regiment, let alone run a country. They also lacked the modesty to comprehend this.

In addition to political instability, the large army also created major economic problems. To pay the recurrent expenditure on the armed forces, the South Vietnamese government was committed to accepting indefinite American aid on a large scale, including the import of subsidized consumer goods in order to generate local piastre funds to pay the army wage bill. For a young independent country to be so completely dependent on foreign aid is both politically and psychologically a misfortune. Similarly, the American commitment to the army was not one that could easily be terminated. It put both sides firmly on the hook and allowed for no flexibility in the provision of aid.

On the civilian side it had further effects. A powerful army naturally attracted all the best young men into its officer ranks. With the army getting the cream, the remaining government services had to make do with skimmed milk. When the insurgency broke out, it soon became apparent that the standard of officials to carry out the civil functions of government, particularly in the provinces, was too low, and army officers were transferred to take their places. By the end of 1964, out of nearly three hundred province and district chiefs, there was hardly a civilian left.

A large army requires a lot of supporting specialized services, including engineers and hospitals. In a country where there were insufficient trained personnel to staff a civilian service, there was now a requirement to support two such services. This would not have been so bad during the insurgency if, for example, the military hospitals had been prepared to treat other than military personnel. However, not even wounded Civil Guard or Self-Defence Corps casualties were admitted, let alone any civilians. In other fields such as information, radio and psychological warfare, the army also usurped civilian functions and tried to make amends by promoting what was called 'civic action'. What in effect was happening was that the army, organized on conventional lines to defeat a foreign invader and to occupy and administer a foreign country, was attempting to do almost exactly that in its own country. This created a completely wrong attitude and led to operations and actions which might just have been excusable as acts of war if carried out in enemy territory. The one vital aspect of civic action which the army failed to develop was good, strict, disciplined behaviour towards its own population. Without that, all assistance or other good works in the rural areas which the army can so admirably provide for the population, and which would contribute generally to better relationships, are so much eyewash.

The conventional organization of the army led naturally to operations of a conventional type. This was not helped by the constant changes amongst the corps and divisional commanders, all of whom wished to make their name with a quick, spectacular military victory. Unless there is a strong overriding authority directing the war, a young inexperienced officer appointed to a division thinks immediately in terms of

divisional operations. Time and time again the following type
of report would appear in the newspapers: 'A two-day
operation involving some 1,200 Vietnamese troops against a
Viet Cong stronghold twenty-five miles north of Saigon ended
early Wednesday with practically no results. Military sources
said one Viet Cong woman was captured and one friendly
soldier was killed by sniper fire in the operation'. Not all
reports were quite so frank.

A British General in Malaya, commanding an area equivalent to a division, was once asked what he considered the
role of a divisional commander to be. He replied: 'As far as I
can see, the only thing a divisional commander has to do in
this sort of war is to go round seeing that the troops have got
their beer!' He had got it right.

The conventional command structure also led to a lack of
initiative in the junior ranks. An insurgency is a junior commander's war, especially in its early stages, but no junior
commander would dare to take action without superior orders,
preferably written. I often put the question to Vietnamese
officers 'If you were ordered to take an infantry company
from A to B and passed a Civil Guard post being attacked by
the Viet Cong, would you go to their assistance or would you
continue to B?' The answer was invariably: 'Continue to B'.
After all, if the junior officer's action had saved the post, the
senior commanders would have taken the credit; but if anything had gone wrong, the junior officer would have got the
blame. The principle of 'carrying the can', under which the
senior officer gets the blame and the junior officer the credit,
was unknown.

The existence of corps and divisional commands extending
over a number of provinces, which in turn were commanded
by junior military officers, led to constant problems over the
control of operations and of intelligence. The province chief as
commander of his sector was subservient to the divisional
commander, but as province chief he was responsible to the
Ministry of the Interior and, in President Diem's day, to the
President himself. The sector command had control over
the para-military forces within the province, and the dual
system of command made combined operations and the

co-ordination of civil and military measures an almost insoluble problem.

A further side-effect of a conventionally equipped army is that weapons designed for conventional war and not suitable for anti-guerilla operations are carried into action. A number of these weapons, such as recoilless rifles, are quite useless against insurgents, but are absolute murder to the government side if they are lost and fall into insurgent hands.

I have dealt with this problem of a large army at some length because I believe that the balance of forces within a country is one of the most vital issues both for the political stability of the country and for ensuring the full co-ordination of civilian measures and military operations in an insurgency. The requirement is for a small, elite, highly disciplined, lightly equipped and aggressive army, with a supporting air force and navy of sufficient capability to make the army highly mobile, so that it can fulfil its proper military role in support of the civil government and in accordance with the five basic principles laid down in this chapter.

need small army

Chapter 5

The Government Cause

BEFORE going on to the roles of the various armed forces or the practical measures required to defeat an insurgency, it is necessary to consider the problems facing a government in its approach to its own people at the outset of an open insurgency. While the insurgent strength both in armed units and in active supporters may be one per cent or less of the population, the hard core on which the government can definitely rely is also likely to be quite a small percentage of the population, perhaps 10 per cent and probably never more than 20 per cent. The remaining 80 or 90 per cent of the population is neutral or near neutral as between the government and the insurgents. If the government strength were more than 20 per cent, and the remainder of the population were not neutral but were ready to support the government, then subversion and selective terrorism would have failed and an insurgency would be doomed from the start. We can therefore assume that the government will have only a loyal hard core and that its main concern will be to win over the vast neutral majority to its own side.

There are three main forces which influence the people of a country: nationalism and national policies, religion and customs, material well-being and progress.

In Malaya the government was fortunate in that the communist movement was identified with the Chinese and was therefore regarded as alien by the Malay population. As a result, Malay nationalism, reinforced as it was by the second force of the Islamic religion, rallied to the government, except for a small movement in Pahang, which, for these very reasons, was half-hearted and quickly collapsed under pressure. The main problem facing the government was to attract and win over the major portion of the Chinese community to its side. This was achieved by the statesmanlike approach of the leading Malays, who were prepared to offer Malayan citizenship to other races on easy terms, and with it a strong political and economic stake in the country, a policy that culminated in the formation of the Alliance Party, which was made up of the leading Malay, Chinese and Indian political associations.

If the harnessing of the nationalist force in Malaya on the side of the government was difficult, it was yet more so in Vietnam owing to the unnatural division of the country at the 17th parallel by the Geneva Agreement of 1954. The Vietnamese nationalism which had defeated the French was itself split in two, and there was little prospect of creating a sense of nationality or nationhood in South Vietnam. Neither North nor South was prepared to renounce its ultimate claim to the other's territory. Reunification was in this sense a more potent force in the Viet Cong's propaganda platform than it was in that of the South Vietnamese government, mainly because it appeared a more credible objective. Even so, more might have been done in South Vietnam to divorce communism from nationalism. Many nationalists who had fought with the Viet Minh rallied to the government's cause against the Viet Cong, and it should have been one of the strongest endeavours of the government to win over more of this group. The very fact that the Viet Cong were given the label 'Viet' even by the government enabled them to retain an element of nationalism in their appeal. This should have been denied them, and more emphasis laid on the communist connection with China, which has always been the traditional foreign enemy of the Vietnamese.

A government must also pay the closest attention to the second main force, that of religion and customs, often complicated by the most conservative superstitions, which more than any other is capable of releasing the strongest emotional feeling. This was a great problem in Malaya, where it was essential to avoid any question of an Islamic religious war against the Chinese which might have united the Chinese community completely against the government. At the first sign of any religious trouble over even a very minor incident, a government must go immediately to action stations to put out the fire and prevent the flames spreading. In Vietnam, where there was probably greater religious tolerance than in Malaya (where Islam was the state religion), it is one of the ironies that a religious incident, in itself probably an accident, should have sparked off the Buddhist controversy which finally split the country and resulted in the downfall of President Diem.

If there was discrimination against the Buddhists in Vietnam in favour of the Catholics, it stemmed partly from the fact that the Catholics generally were better educated and therefore able to take greater material advantage of their opportunities, and partly from the fact that the Catholics were more committed as a whole to the war against the Viet Cong. Many of them had fled as refugees from the North and were established in large new land-resettlement areas in South Vietnam, which they proved themselves ready and able to defend against Viet Cong attack. For this purpose their requirements in arms and other materials were naturally met. A great portion of the blame for the religious controversy must of course go to the President and his family for fanning the flames instead of extinguishing them in the early stages. Even so, when political opposition of a treasonable nature to a government in time of war takes refuge under a religious umbrella, the religion cannot expect to remain immune to political counter-measures. Turbulent priests cannot always claim sanctuary.

However powerful nationalist or religious forces may be, that of material well-being is as strong if not stronger, especially in peasant communities where the family tradition is venerated and the instinctive loyalties are to the advancement of closest relatives. The peasant in Vietnam was vaguely conscious that one of the communists' aims was to capture the rich rice-lands of the Mekong Delta; but he understood more clearly the failures of communism in the agricultural sphere both in China and in North Vietnam, and the communist methods of administering agricultural production through communes and collectivization rather than through peasant farmers. This ran counter to every peasant's ambition to own sufficient land, and to build a house in which his ancestors could be worshipped and his descendants could multiply.

In the sphere of material well-being, all the advantages lie

with the government, which in addition to its own resources
has access to the aid of friendly countries and international
agencies. On the constructive side there are innumerable
projects which cannot fail to make an impact, such as new
schools, hospitals, clinics, rural roads, better water supplies
and even electricity. With more modern methods, great improvements are also possible in basic agricultural production,
and in many cases new crops can be introduced. Even prestige
projects, which may be of questionable economic value, can
play their part in building a sense of national pride. People
like to see four-engined jet airliners landing at their own
airport.

If the government can exploit this field of modern development, it can create a situation in which people will not willingly sacrifice either their present standards of living or their
prospects of future progress. It is at the same time most important to combine this wind of development and progress with an
air of established order. In this respect the greatest importance
should be attached to the Constitution, from which all authority is derived and on which all basic human rights rest.
Constitutions can be amended by due process, but to abrogate
the Constitution, as occurred in Vietnam after the fall of
President Diem, was a fundamental error leading to a state of
continuous instability.

Nor should one underrate the stabilizing influence of such
things as pensions and provident funds, of which the most
striking example is probably the Employees Provident Fund
in Malaya, which was started in 1950. Under this scheme, all
those earning less than a certain sum every month were
required to contribute to the fund, with the employer paying
a fixed percentage and the employee a lesser percentage out
of his wages, the onus of collection being on the employer. The
purpose of the Fund was to meet the problem of old age, no
sickness or unemployment. The benefits were only payable on
reaching the age of 55, on leaving the country for good, or
being permanently disabled or on death. In a young and
growing country the contributions to the Fund are enormous
compared with the benefits that have to be paid out in the
early stages. The intake was soon running at over one hundred

million Malayan dollars a year. This in turn had to be invested by the Board responsible for the Fund, who naturally invested it mainly in government securities, thereby giving the government a vast reservoir of money for capital development. Every contributor received an annual statement, and when, after a few years, a rubber tapper could see that he was worth several thousand dollars invested in the government and knew that it would be paid when due, it is easy to guess whose side he was on.

In underdeveloped and newly independent countries, which are the most likely to be threatened by insurgency, there has been a tendency to establish strong central governments of an authoritarian nature with some concessions to democratic procedures. In both Malaya and India, where the rule of law prevails and where there is the greatest acceptance of democratic principles, both governments have had overwhelming parliamentary majorities. Where this has not obtained, there has been a further tendency to establish one-party rule and to crush all opposition. This is because leading personalities become identified with the state itself, and also because the concept of a loyal opposition is incomprehensible. This does not necessarily mean that such personalities lack political support. In Vietnam, for example, however rigged the presidential elections may have been, I have no doubt that President Diem would still have got a majority, particularly from the rural population, which would have given great satisfaction to any western President or Prime Minister. What could not be tolerated in the circumstances of the country at the time was evidence in the voting of a large, if disunited, opposition which sought not just the constitutional overthrow of the government but the assassination of the President and his closest supporters. The crushing of opposition inevitably leads to conspiracy, from which the threat can often seem greater than would be the case with an open opposition. But for a government to function with a loyal opposition on the lines of western democracy must take a very considerable time. It requires the build-up of respected institutions—judicial, legislative and administrative—together with many unwritten but well-understood traditions and conventions. This process is likely to take even longer in an agricultural and peasant community (with which the source of political power should lie) because of the peasant's innate suspicion of any central government and his general desire to be left alone.

One cannot therefore easily parade democracy as it is understood in the West as the ideological counter to communism. If an authoritarian government can still build up an image based on the rule of law and the execution of constructive and progressive national policies on which it can be judged by its performance, then it is possible to establish in people's minds an equation something like this:

legality + construction + results   = the government
illegality + destruction + promises = the insurgents

This is likely to make much more sense to a peasant than repeated statements that democracy is better than communism.

This does not mean that no attempt should be made to build up the democratic processes, starting preferably at the grass roots in the villages of the countryside, but it cannot easily be done in an insurgent situation. Security must come first. There was the case of a new village in Johore in Malaya when the election of the village committee was held prematurely, before full security had been achieved. There was no trouble over the voting, but at the end of the day when the votes were being counted, the candidates stood there in fear and trembling. As soon as the results were announced, the successful candidates rushed from the hall and caught the next bus for Singapore. They regarded their election as a sentence of death and were not seen again until they were certain that their lives were no longer in danger from terrorist action.

This was an individual case, and elsewhere the formation of elected village committees worked so well that they were later formally constituted as Local Councils, with responsibility for minor administrative matters and with power to levy local taxes of a rating nature. This system of local government, including also Town and Municipal Councils, provided the political experience (political parties were soon contesting the seats) and established the democratic procedures on which national elections could subsequently be based.

Finally, if its cause is to be effective, the government must demonstrate both its determination and its capacity to win. These are the foundations of popular support. After all, there are not many backers for a losing side. At the height of an insurgency, if the issue is evenly balanced, neither the government nor the insurgent cause is a matter of great importance. At that stage there is only one political question: 'Who is going to win?'

Chapter 6

The Administrative Structure

IF the government performance is going to be effective and keep pace with the aspirations of the people, while at the same time creating an atmosphere of order and stability, the main essential is to establish a sound administrative structure. The best of plans, programmes and policies will remain nothing but good intentions unless the machinery exists to execute them so that they make their impact throughout the country.

In order to ensure cohesion within the government and co-ordination between its ministries, it is highly desirable to establish a Cabinet system of government with well-defined procedures. The essentials of a Cabinet system and its great advantages are that the decisions of government are not taken hastily and extempore, but with full knowledge of the background and of the arguments for and against any particular policy; and that the decisions, once taken, are the collective responsibility of all Ministers of the government and are not open to subsequent questioning or repudiation by any individual Minister. As a result, the decisions which are taken are those which have the best chance of proving right under the test of time, and the country becomes conscious that the decisions of its government are fair, honest and dependable and are in the best interests of the country as a whole.

All major policy questions, and in particular all legislation, taxation and expenditure, should be submitted to the Cabinet. Even though a particular subject concerns only one Ministry, it may be of such importance that it requires the approval and support of the Cabinet as a whole. All Ministers require the support of their colleagues for their policies, and, conversely, when touring the country, may frequently have to answer questions on, or support, their colleagues' policies; if these have been discussed and approved in Cabinet, they are in a position to do so.

The prerequisites for the establishment of a Cabinet system are the clear definition of responsibilities between the various Ministries and Departments of government, the creation and training of a small Cabinet Secretariat, and the institution of regular meetings and a timetable within which the machinery can work. The first of these, definition of responsibilities, is essential in order to avoid overlapping in cases when more than one Department may be concerned with the same subject, and, equally, to avoid gaps when a subject which ought to occupy the attention of the government is neglected because each Department or Ministry assumes another to be dealing with it. In this way all Ministers are associated with all major government policy decisions and can direct the actions of their respective Ministries accordingly. Similarly, all officials concerned are aware of the government's decisions and can carry out the government's policy in the knowledge that Ministers have accepted full responsibility for it.

In Malaya, a Cabinet system was early established, based on the Executive Council of the British High Commissioner, and was followed by the Member system, under which members of the Council became responsible for certain departments of the government, and this was in full working order by the time Malaya became independent in 1957. When I asked one of President Diem's Ministers in 1962 how the system worked in Vietnam, he replied that a Cabinet meeting was normally called at short notice, and then only to receive a three-hour lecture from the President himself. Ministerial responsibilities were not defined, and the President, if dissatisfied with the functioning of a particular department, instead of reforming the department or replacing its head, merely transferred some of its responsibilities to another official or department, often without informing those concerned. This guaranteed that all the wires got nicely crossed.

In my view there are two basic aims in devising a suitable administrative structure for the executive side of the government (that is excluding the legislature and judiciary). These are to establish and maintain the closest contact between the government and the people, and to provide a simple and efficient organization which is economic in both personnel and expenditure. In a newly independent country which is both underdeveloped and facing the threat of communist aggression and subversion, it is also essential that the administrative structure should provide for a strong central national government, which can prepare and implement national policies throughout the country and, through them, develop national unity, national consciousness and national loyalty.

In Vietnam there were five levels at which the administrative structure had to be considered: national, province, district, village (including towns and cities) and hamlet. The two most important of these levels were national and village, but the most difficult to fit into the structure was the province.

At the national level, the two important points arising from Cabinet procedure and organization are, first, that the Cabinet should be responsible for approving all national policies on every aspect of the country's government, because it is these policies which provide the necessary direction to the ministries in their respective fields; and, second, that the responsibilities of each ministry should be very clearly defined so that there are no gaps and no duplication. This listing of responsibilities will automatically show each ministry where there must be co-ordination with other ministries in formulating and carrying out policy. For example, it is no good the Ministry of Health proposing twenty new hospitals in one year if the Ministry of Public Works requires three years to build them, and the Ministry of Finance can only provide the funds over five years.

A ministry which has received its general direction on policy from the Cabinet is then responsible for the practical execution of that policy throughout the country. The manner in which the approved policy is phased, and planned, becomes in its turn the ministry's policy, to be put into effect by the various departments and their officials under each ministry. With regard to a ministry, there are generally two types of organization. If a ministry has a large number of departments (for example, the Ministry of Public Works may have Public Works, Ports, Railways, Posts and Telecommunications), it is best to have a small ministry, composed almost entirely of civil servants, advised on technical matters by the respective heads of department. Where, however, a ministry has a single department, as is often the case with Education, the ministry itself should be integrated with the head office of the department. This also works surprisingly well with Defence.

The technical and professional departments are the main executive units of the government, responsible for giving practical effect on the ground to the policies laid down. It follows that, depending on their particular field of activity, it is the departments who provide the main body of officials distributed throughout the country at the various levels in the administrative structure. At the national level, and in most cases at the province level also, a number of civil servants will be required in the departments for general administrative and clerical work, in order to avoid wasting trained technical officers on such tasks. It is most important that the departmental chain of command should be maintained from the head of a national department right down to the department's lowest official in the field. I particularly advocate national government departments because they are more efficient and economic, both in trained personnel and in expenditure, and because they are the most effective way of producing the results expected from a national policy.

The Education Department provides a good example. In an underdeveloped country, where the population is young and education is a primary requirement, it is essential to have a national education policy as one of the means of welding the population together, and of ensuring that all talented children, however poor they may be, have opportunities of higher education, including university. Also, only when it is dealt with on a national scale, is it possible to solve the problem of establishing and training a good body of teachers. They should be paid by the government. Not only does this provide a degree of government control over them (which is important in circumstances where they are a target of communist subversion) but it also gives them greater security in their employment and prospects of promotion. If local authorities are given responsibility for any of the major functions of government such as education, it will be found that they can employ only the poorest quality (if they can get any profes-

advocates Brit type gov — national govaling

sionally qualified officials at all), and that the services provided for the people are of the lowest standard.

While it may have been desirable for military and security reasons in respect of sector commands to increase the number of provinces in South Vietnam, it would have been far better for simplicity of administration, and reasons of economy both in personnel and in expenditure, to have reduced the administrative provinces to a maximum of thirty, and preferably less. It is difficult for a national department in the capital to maintain the necessary contact with, and supervision over, more than this number of sub-offices. If there are too many provincial offices, the requirement may well arise for the establishment of regional departmental offices between the national level and the provincial level. This should, if possible, be avoided, since it is administratively wasteful and creates an unnecessary tier in the structure. It also tends to encourage a regional autonomy in conflict with the national interest and national policy. There are, of course, special cases when there may be a need for regional offices: for example, in the case of the National Police Force, which will probably have a wider coverage of the country than any other department; or, in the case of small departments, such as Geological Survey, which will only require three or four regional offices throughout the country and do not need an office in each province. In other cases it may also be necessary to use certain provincial offices for stationing specialized officers with a regional function covering more than one province. This would apply to certain medical and agricultural specialists.

The provincial head of a departmental office should be directly responsible to the national head of department for carrying out the departmental policy in his province. He should not be responsible to the Province Chief (or Governor), whose role I shall discuss later. Where the department has further sub-offices in the province, normally at district level, then the provincial head of department is responsible for their running and supervision. All the officials of the department in that province should look to him alone for the necessary guidance and leadership in carrying out departmental policy in the field.

The key figure, however, in the administration of a primarily rural country is the Province Chief, linking, as he does, the two levels at which the political direction of the government is exerted, namely the national and the village level. He is the local symbol of the authority of the national government, and is normally responsible for collecting the taxes, payable to the national Exchequer, while his Treasury, conversely, acts as banker for the ministries and departments with offices in his province. He exercises any powers that have been conferred on him by legislation as the local representative of the central government—for instance as a licensing authority—and will at least have a supervisory, and in some cases a statutory, role in the establishing and running of local authorities in his province, such as town and village councils. With regard to departmental offices in his province, he is the planning co-ordinator, and is responsible for the smooth working relationship between them so as to ensure balanced progress, but he should not command them or have direct authority over them.

In addition to these general duties, the Province Chief ought to have responsibility for one important specific subject in his province. This should be land. It is his office which should be responsible for all aspects of the government's approved land policy, including land reform, registration of titles, land use and development, land taxes and the acquisition of land on behalf of the government. This brings him into the closest contact with the people on the subject dearest to their hearts. It also provides an excellent focal point for the co-ordination of all government policy in the province, because roads, hospitals and schools cannot be built without first acquiring land.

In short, the personal qualities required of a Province Chief are of a high order. He must be politically independent, and ready to carry out loyally changes of policy resulting from changes of government, whilst ensuring stability and the continuity of essential public services without whose maintenance political changes might lead to chaos. He must be devoted to his public, and able to get on with them individually, inspiring confidence in his own judgement and honesty, and, through himself, in both the government of the day and government in general. He should be constantly watchful, on the one hand, over the life of the community (law and order, economic, political and social stability), and on the other over the functioning of the whole government machine, making it his special charge to safeguard the rights of individuals and minority groups. This is a role essentially for a mature civil servant, able to weigh up when to let the administrative machine run by itself, and when and how far to intervene without obstructing it.

Just as the number of provinces should be limited, so with districts, the ideal number probably being about five for each province. The District Chief is no more than an extension of the Province Chief, and is of great importance because of his close contact with the people and the machinery of government at the lowest level. Few government departments will have offices below the province level, but at district headquarters the National Police, Agriculture and Medical and Public Works may be represented as government services are expanded. The National Police is likely to be the only department which has police stations or posts below the district level. All departmental offices working at district level, including visiting officials from the province, will take their instructions from their provincial head of department and not from the District Chief, who will, however, be responsible for co-ordinating their work in his district. The important function of the District Chief will be the establishment and supervision of village councils, and the provision of government assistance to them. It is a post which should be sought after and held by all young administrative civil servants for a tour of at least three years before they can qualify for promotion. It is a great test of character, initiative and judgement.

The village in Vietnam, as in many other countries, has traditionally been a strong administrative unit, and it was most important that it should be retained as such and so organized that it could give the people themselves a part to play in the running of their own local affairs. A village unit, consisting of a population of about 5,000, normally contained four or five hamlets. This should be regarded as a minimum size, and there is no reason why a village should not cover a much larger population of between 10,000 and 20,000 people. But if it is to be a cohesive unit, the people should have the same interests in common so that the necessary community spirit can be built up.

In order that the people can play their part in local affairs, village councils should be statutorily established, with between five and ten members, depending on the size of the village. The chairman of the council should become the Village Chief, and other members should be given responsibilities for specific subjects. It will be necessary for the council to have a clerk, who may be either part-time or full-time, depending on the size of the village. The council should have powers to make local by-laws and regulations, covering the administration of the village area, and to raise simple taxes, for example a house tax, licensing of shops, market stalls, etc. The council should work on an annual budget, but it will be found that in nearly all cases the village revenue will be inadequate, and the council will therefore need some financial assistance by way of a grant from the national government. For this reason, annual budgets should be approved by the Province Chief. Shortage of funds will dictate that the responsibilities of village councils should be limited. They cannot be expected to carry out those services in their village area which ought to be the responsibility of the national government. For example, all through-roads and major canals should be the responsibility of the national government, and the village council should only be responsible for minor roads and tracks and small canals. The national government should also be responsible for the National Police, schools and medical facilities through the respective government departments. While some facilities, therefore, will be provided direct by the government, there will be many cases in which a joint effort will be required, particularly in respect of self-help projects of a capital nature, where the government provides the material and the village provides the labour. This concept of community development was well understood in Vietnam, and can be extended into many aspects of village community life.

I was not in favour of establishing hamlet councils for administrative purposes, though they are required in an insurgency to organize the security of a hamlet and to help identify the people with their own defence. Hamlets are normally too small to be a viable administrative unit, and lack the individual talent which would be capable of making them work. The resources of a hamlet are also far too small to undertake many of the projects, which are better organized at village level. It is, however, desirable that there should be a Hamlet Chief, elected for a period of two to three years. He should not be one of the hamlet representatives on the village council, but should be a separate official, so that he can be a contact between the people of the hamlet and all superior authorities, including the village council, in their operations at hamlet level. For this duty, he should receive a small salary, and this should be paid by the central government.

The administrative structure which I have described deals almost entirely with the permanent officials of the civil service and the government technical departments in ministries and provincial administrations, who take their policy instructions from the elected representatives of the people at the national level. It is in my view undesirable to insert further elected tiers into this structure, for example an elected council at the province level. Such councils would merely be a façade unless they were given the normal powers of an elected body to make local laws and raise local taxes. If such powers were given to a province council, it would tend to build up a provincial or territorial autonomy, which would undermine, and could obstruct, the authority of the central government. The democratic principle is subjected to its greatest strain when local authorities are elected from a different party than that controlling the central government. For the sake of unity and consistency of progress throughout the country, it is strongly to be recommended that the elective principle should be confined to the national level, where policy is directed, and to the lowest level, such as municipal, town, and village councils and the Hamlet Chief, where the people need to be intimately connected with day-to-day local affairs.

I feel very strongly that in an underdeveloped country the insertion of any elected politicians into an administrative structure, or even changes of personnel as a result of political appointments, will only weaken the structure and tend to bring government itself into disrepute. Apart from the fact that politicians generally lack administrative experience, they are subject to pressures and influences which affect their judgement and sometimes lead to discrimination and corruption.

Taxation is another good reason for confining elections to the national and the village level; while 'no taxation without representation' is a frequently quoted principle of democracy, the converse is equally true, that taxation is the most important responsibility of a representative government. No government can function at all without revenue, or retain popular support unless taxation is equitably imposed and conscientiously collected. For simplicity and efficiency of administration, it is a great advantage if the major direct and indirect taxes throughout the country are imposed, collected and controlled by the national government. This also results in a fairer and more flexible distribution of expenditure, so that the richer areas can be taxed to help develop the poorer areas, thereby expanding the whole economy of the country. If taxes are mainly regional, the rich areas become richer and the poor areas remain poor. This argument does not apply at the village level, where local village taxes will in any case be very limited and inadequate for their purpose. By making grants to villages in accordance with their needs, the government can achieve a fairer and more flexible distribution of the national funds allocated for this purpose.

It may take many years, perhaps a generation, to build up the desired administrative structure, and efficient professional and administrative services to staff it. This was one of the chief problems facing President Diem, who discussed it with me for the whole of one afternoon. He particularly admired the administrative organization in former British territories. He said of the Americans that all they could give him were enormous, complicated charts. He added: 'I have thousands of officers sitting in chairs on charts. But how do you make it all work?'

There are, I think, two service principles which it is essential to instil in all government officials, right from the start, if an administrative structure is to work. The first is that an

administration will function effectively only if it has the respect and co-operation of the people. This respect and co-
operation must be earned, not compelled, by the behaviour
and helpfulness of all officials in their dealings with the public.
The second is that there must be complete confidence between
senior and junior officials. Junior officials must be supported
all the way up the line by senior officials above them, so that
initiative and keenness in carrying out their duty are encouraged, and mistakes are rectified, not covered up. It is the
senior official who is responsible for, and must take the blame
for, his junior's mistakes or inefficiency. The English expression for this is 'carrying the can'. These two principles must
govern the attitude of mind of all officials, both to the public
whom they serve and to each other. Only an administrative
structure built up in this way, with permanent officials to staff
it, can provide the framework for an effective and acceptable
alternative system of government to communism.

At a subsequent interview with Nguyen Dinh Thuan,
President Diem's senior Secretary of State, I repeated these
two service principles, and also stated that a government had
to be on guard against the further weakness of a government
officer who could cruise through thirty years of public service
at his desk without doing a single constructive act. Thuan
laughed, and replied: 'You know us too well!'

The existence of a sound administrative structure, although
complicated by a federal system of government, was perhaps
the greatest advantage which Malaya had over South Vietnam. The deficiency in South Vietnam was further com-
pounded by temporary *ad hoc* measures designed to bolster
particular weaknesses. The worst of these was the formation
of thousands of crash trained 'cadres' to work in the villages
and to carry the government's (or more often the particular
minister's) message to the people. This was about all they had
to offer. The real answer should have been the longer training
of lower-rank officials from government departments in the
practical and technical aspects of departmental work, such as
teachers, nurses, veterinary assistants, agricultural assistants
and public works foremen, who could have produced practical
benefits and results.

This emphasis on the administrative structure concerns not only the country itself but also those other countries which support it, both in development programmes and in counter-insurgency measures. The value derived from that support will vary in direct ratio to the efficiency of the administration. In the ideal situation, when the administration is 100 per cent efficient, then the supporting countries will obtain one dollar's worth of results for every dollar of their aid. In conditions of anarchy, they will merely be pouring their dollars down the drain. This accounts for the fact that, where the existing administration is thoroughly inefficient, the visible results of aid are Mercedes cars, foreign travel and fancy wedding receptions.

* * *

When an insurgency breaks out, the question immediately arises of how far the government should alter its normal administrative structure in order to meet the needs of the situation. Provided that the government meets the third basic principle and produces an overall plan which includes all political, military, economic, administrative, police and other measures which have a bearing on the insurgency, it is desirable to limit any re-organization, and to avoid creating any new machinery except in so far as it is necessary to ensure co-ordination of effort, quicker decisions than are normally possible in a bureaucracy and closer supervision of their execution.

In order to provide for firm government direction of the campaign, it is advisable to set up, under the Cabinet, a form of National War Council, which will be responsible for all major policy decisions on the conduct of the campaign. The chairman of this Council should be the Prime Minister, and its members should be three or four other ministers, including the Minister of Defence, the Minister of the Interior, the Minister of Finance (money is always involved) and the Minister of Information, as well as the senior military officers and civilian officials concerned with the conduct of the war. These last should consist of the heads of the three armed services and of the police force, one or two senior permanent officials from the Ministry of Defence or the Ministry of the Interior and the head of the intelligence organization.

Just as with the Cabinet itself, this Council should meet formally and as frequently as may be required. To start with, weekly meetings may be necessary, but as the campaign progresses, the intervals can grow longer. Towards the end of the insurgency in Malaya, this Council was meeting about once every three months. All proposals put before the Council should be in the form of written memoranda, so that the full implications of all policies can be considered. The Council's decisions should be recorded in writing, and all departments of the government, including the armed forces, concerned with the decisions should be informed in writing, so that all officers and officials know exactly what their duties and responsibilities are. Under no circumstances should the Council play it off the cuff. This only leads to confusion and encourages disputes at lower levels as to what the policy really is. As a result, the government will begin to lose its control over the direction of the campaign. It is also advisable that the government should appoint as the senior official member of the Council a Director of Operations, preferably the senior military officer available to the government, who should be responsible for the day-to-day direction of the war and supervision of the execution of the policies approved by the Council. He should have a very small staff, including a small forward-planning staff, composed of military, police and civilian officers, not exceeding a total of ten, to assist him in his duties.

I stress the smallness of this staff very strongly because there are two basic principles involved. First, the Director of Operations is not a commander. The normal chains of command both in the armed forces and in government departments should continue to operate in the ordinary way, with instructions being issued through the ordinary channels of command in accordance with the decisions of the National War Council and such further implementing directions as may be given by the Director of Operations. Second, ministries, military headquarters and government departments must do all the work for which they are responsible. Neither the Director of Operations nor the Ministry of Defence should become involved with work that is by rights the responsibility of other departments just because the measures concerned have a counter-insurgency bias. If the Director of Operations is not adamant about this, he will end up running an entirely separate government, including the Railways!

Once policies have been decided, their implementation should be left to the departments and military headquarters concerned. To ensure complete co-ordination it is desirable for the Director of Operations to have a standing committee of the senior officials involved, preferably confined to those on the National War Council, with others attending only for the particular problem that concerns them.

In the same way at a lower level, particularly at that of the province, a small committee should be formed, consisting of the senior civilian officer, senior military officer and senior police officer of the province, which should meet regularly, and be attended by such other officers as may be concerned with any particular item, in order to implement the policies approved by the National War Council. All members of these committees will have received their instructions on the subject through their normal chains of command. 'War by Committee' is frequently derided, but the system works if it is understood that the committees do not override the normal chains of command, but are there to ensure greater co-ordination in the execution of policy by reaching agreement on how it should be implemented in the particular area for which the committee is responsible. If agreement cannot be reached, that is partly what the Director of Operations is for. He is in a position to settle such disputes, and by referring the matter to the appropriate authority, he can see that any difficult or offending officer is suitably relegated. When one or two examples have been made, a surprising unity of effort is soon encouraged.

Chapter 7

Intelligence

'LET'S go out and kill some Viet Cong, then we can worry about intelligence.' This remark by a newly arrived General lends weight to the old gag that there are only two types of generals in counter-insurgency—those who haven't yet learnt it and those who never will! Fortunately there are some exceptions.

If subversion is the main threat, starting as it does well before an open insurgency and continuing through it and even afterwards, it follows that within the government the intelligence organization is of paramount importance. In fact I would go so far as to say that no government can hope to defeat a communist insurgent movement unless it gives top priority to, and is successful in, building up such an organization. The use of the terms 'subversion' and 'insurgency' tends to suggest that the threat is rather ill-defined and abstract. This is not the case. The threat to the internal security of the country arises entirely from the actions and intentions of individual men and women engaged in that subversion or insurgency. It is the individual who plans to subvert others to carry out illegal acts against the state, and it is the individual, acting singly or in a group or in an armed unit, who carries out subversive or insurgent acts. It must therefore be the aim of the intelligence organization to identify such individuals, with a view to eliminating them or at least preventing them from carrying out illegal acts against the security of the country. It is not the aim of the intelligence organization merely to penetrate the insurgent movement. Its aim, inside its own country, must be the total eradication of the threat. For this purpose the organization must be directed to obtain the fullest details of the identity of each individual communist. Just as armed guerillas can conceal themselves amongst the peasants, so do communist terrorists who penetrate the villages and towns conceal themselves amongst the population. They have a well-established security system, and realize that they become vulnerable if their identity is disclosed. This is one of the reasons why they use so many aliases, the cell system and other similar measures. To defeat them requires a very delicate machine staffed by well-trained and highly experienced intelligence officers.

Ideally there should be one single organization responsible for all security intelligence within the country. If there is more than one, it is almost impossible to define the respective responsibilities of each organization or to devise any means of co-ordinating their activities. All sorts of things will start to go wrong. For example, agents, especially the less reliable, will get themselves onto the payroll of several organizations and feed them the same unreliable information. Such information seemingly confirmed from different sources will be accepted as authentic. The different organizations will withhold information from one another in order to exploit it and obtain the credit for themselves. A promising line of intelligence promoted by one organization may well be cut inadvertently, or even intentionally, by another organization. Mutual suspicion and jealousies will arise, quite likely with the result that the separate organizations merely end up by spying on each other. The intelligence, on which government plans should be based, will be both patchy and unreliable.

The best organization to be responsible for all internal security intelligence is the special branch of the police force rather than a completely separate organization. It is a great advantage if intelligence officers have police powers and are able to call when necessary on the other branches of the police force for support and assistance in developing their intelligence network. The police force is a static organization reaching out into every corner of the country and will have had long experience of close contact with the population. If it can possibly be avoided, the army should not be responsible for internal security intelligence. The army will have had little concern with subversion before the open insurgency breaks out; it will have had very limited experience of contacting the people, particularly rural communities, which are inherently suspicious of troops; and its units are always liable to be redeployed throughout the country in accordance with the situation. Any intelligence lines which these units may have established are then immediately uprooted. In an insurgency the army is one of the main consumers of intelligence, but it should not be a collector except in so far as its units obtain tactical intelligence through their operations. If a special branch intelligence organization is established throughout the country, the army, through its own intelligence branch, can hook into it at any point where its units are stationed, thereby receiving the information on which to base operations and at the same time feeding into the organization the tactical intelligence which its units acquire.

Perhaps nearly as bad as no intelligence organization, or a multiplicity of intelligence organizations, is an overloaded one. This can lead to a situation in which every hole has a terrier down it. All are wagging their tails and barking to be fed, with the net result that you have no clue which hole has a rat down it. Intelligence officers, like terriers, must be trained to cover many holes, to ignore those that are vacant and to bark only when there is a rat down one.

One of the main arguments, if not the only one, against the establishment of a single internal security intelligence organization is that too much power and knowledge is entrusted to too few people, and that few governments would be inclined to take this risk. My only comment is that, if a government has so few people that it can trust, it is anyway not likely to last long as a government, even without an insurgency.

As in all other aspects of insurgency, the intelligence organization, however good, must still limit its targets and not disperse its effort too widely. The primary target should be the contact points between the communist subversive organization working in the villages and towns, and the guerilla units outside the population (as already shown by the heavy line in the diagram on page 56). This is not the place to go into intelligence techniques; it is enough to say that by picking up these contacts, the intelligence organization will obtain leads inwards into the subversive organization and also outwards into the guerilla units. This will enable it to build up a complete picture of the whole insurgent movement, including the iden-

tity and names of all wanted persons. Intelligence is rather like
a ladder, which must be built from the bottom rung upwards.
As you progress, the rungs become more and more fragile
but the view gets better and better. If a rung breaks, your
falling weight is likely to break all the rungs below it, and
you will have to start all over again. Impatience to reach
the top of the ladder often means that you will never get there.

The imposition of control measures on the movement of
people and supplies, which is described in Chapter 12, is
of great assistance to an intelligence organization in discover-
ing the underground members of the subversive organization.
If these members are to do their work, then at some time or
another they must inevitably break or evade some of the
control measures, and this helps to reveal their identity. For
example, if a food supplier in possession of a perfectly genuine
identity card is to make contact with a guerilla unit or move
the supplies which he has collected, constant checks maintained
by the police under the direction of the intelligence organization will eventually reveal him, and a whole cell may then
be eliminated.

Apart from information provided by agents and ordinary
members of the population, the two main sources of intelligence are captured documents and surrendered or captured
enemy personnel. Documents seldom reveal information
which can be immediately exploited by operations, but they
do help to build up a complete picture of the insurgent
movement, and contain a tremendous amount of detailed
information about individuals in it. This is even more the case
with regard to captured or surrendered personnel. Whatever
the circumstances of the insurgency, there will nearly always
be some people who are prepared to surrender for one reason
or another and join the government side. Well-treated and
carefully interrogated, sometimes over a long period, they
reveal a tremendous amount of information. A situation
gradually develops whereby any later individual who is captured or surrenders can then be interrogated on the basis of a
mass of information already available to the intelligence
organization. This shocks the truth out of him far more effectively than torture.

If there is a well-publicized standard rate of rewards for information leading to the killing or capture of terrorists and the recovery of weapons, the natural cupidity of many members of the population soon involves them in the hunt, particularly if they know that their identity will not be revealed and that they will be paid on the nail in cash in accordance with results. A half-rate of the standard rewards can be offered to surrendered terrorists who may later find themselves in a position to open up a small coffee shop in a distant town (where they may still be of great value to the intelligence organization). There is nothing like establishing prospects whereby an individual can go from terrorist to capitalist in two easy moves!

As the intelligence builds up, so more effective operations can be planned. This shows up at once in the ratio of contacts to operations. An increase in the contact rate is the purpose of intelligence, whereas kills depend on training, tactics and good shooting. The absence of such an intelligence organization accounts for the lamentable contact rate in Vietnam, where, in 1964, some typical monthly figures for minor operations (less than a battalion but down to squad size) are as follows:

59,996 operations	· · ·	451 contacts
72,794 operations	· · ·	406 contacts
73,726 operations	· · ·	491 contacts

This gives an average of about one contact to every 150 operations. Naturally, in major operations in which a battalion or more was employed, the contact rate was much higher, nearly one to every two operations, but the contact itself was frequently a very minor one. In an insurgency it is not the major operations that defeat the insurgents. It is a high rate of contact in minor operations, based on good intelligence and resulting perhaps in only one or two kills to each contact. These soon add up.

It is the presence of a well-established internal security intelligence organization which now accounts for the rapid elimination of Indonesian parties landing on the coast of Malaya. Such incursions are immediately reported, and contact is frequently made in a matter of hours.

Good intelligence leads to more frequent and more rapid contacts. More contacts lead to more kills. These in turn lead to greater confidence in the population, resulting in better intelligence and still more contacts and kills. That, General, is why you should first worry about intelligence.

Chapter 8

Information Services

AS with intelligence, so with the information services. There needs to be a closely integrated effort so that the government speaks with one voice. The task naturally falls into two categories: information work directed at the insurgents (i.e. psychological warfare) and information work directed at the public. Not only do the two go together, but the first requires very close co-operation with the intelligence organization. The aim of the first is to reduce the will of the insurgents to fight and to encourage surrenders, while the aim of the second is to rally the population to the side of the government and to encourage positive support for the government in its campaign.

The main base of a successful psychological warfare campaign will depend on a clear and precise government surrender policy towards the insurgents. Such a policy has three main aims: (1) to encourage insurgent surrenders; (2) to sow dissension between insurgent rank-and-file and their leaders; and (3) to create an image of government both to the insurgents and to the population which is both firm and efficient but at the same time just and generous.

The first and most important requirement is to decide the exact and precise terms of the government surrender offer. It must be both attractive and fair but not too lenient or vague. It should be remembered that an offer can easily be improved later, as circumstances may require, but it is not so easy to reduce the terms of an offer without prejudicing the government's good faith. In the early stages of the campaign an amnesty should not be offered. There are two objections, one legal and the other political. 'Amnesty' is a term which in law implies the granting of a free pardon to all persons for any crimes they have committed. Moreover, if an amnesty continues indefinitely, it may easily imply a free pardon for crimes not yet committed. No government can go as far as that without forfeiting respect or without looking as if the offer is made from a position of weakness. The political objection is that the announcement of an amnesty could quickly be exploited by the communists as propaganda for a peace offensive of their own, on the lines that their high command accepts the government's offer on behalf of all its units and is ready to stop the shooting in exchange for recognition of the communist party as a legitimate political party with equal rights. The Malayan Communist Party represented the 1955 amnesty offer in precisely this fashion, only being thwarted by the government's firm stand against it because at the time the government was in a position of overwhelming strength. A moment may come towards the end of a campaign, if the communist forces are crippled (with both their military and their political potential consequently reduced), when an amnesty offer for a strictly limited period might have decisive results. This can only be judged at the time.

In the early stages a definite and precise surrender offer is required, which must be publicized by the government and apply to the whole country. It might be on the following lines:

TO ALL PERSONS WHO HAVE JOINED THE INSURGENTS

Many of your comrades, realizing that they have been deceived and misled by their communist leaders, have rallied to the Government during the past few months and have been well treated. The Government now makes the following offer to all those bearing arms against the Government and those who support them:

1. If you now come in and co-operate with the Government, you will be given fair treatment and the opportunity to 'self-renew' and to rejoin your families.
2. If you have committed murder or other brutal crimes against civilian members of the population, you may be required to stand your trial but your sentence will depend upon the manner in which you subsequently co-operate with the Government.
3. This offer does not apply to those who are captured in operations, but if such persons subsequently co-operate with the Government, then they may be accorded the same terms as those who 'rally' voluntarily.

Signed..

This offer should be signed by the highest authority, preferably the President or the Prime Minister; and if the message is printed on a leaflet, there should be added some such instruction as 'When you come in, bring this leaflet with you as a safe-conduct pass. You will be well treated by all members of the Government forces'.

An offer of this nature is brief, clear and firm. In the early stage of an insurgency it does not promise too much and is obviously not made by a side which is losing. It draws a distinction between those who are responsible for brutal crimes (normally the leaders) and those who are not, thereby sowing one useful seed of dissension. Once having been made, the offer itself does not need to be repeated too frequently. It is preferable that all successive publicity and psychological warfare appeals should be directed to units and individuals locally, but in no circumstances should any such appeal go beyond the government offer. Terminology is also important, and the word 'surrender' should not be used. A suitable vernacular word is required, to imply that the individual insurgent has taken the wrong road and now has a chance to take the right one. It is desirable to get across the idea that individual insurgents have been deceived and misled by the leaders into joining the communist side, and that the government recognizes that it is not their fault but the fault of those leaders. Terms like 'prisoner of war' should also be avoided for obvious reasons.

The absolutely vital factor in a surrender campaign will not be so much the offer itself but how in fact individual insurgents are treated when they do surrender. It is on this treatment that the success of the surrender campaign will depend. It alone will provide the proof to the insurgent that the government offer is both genuine and acceptable. At the same time it will build up the image of the government which it is important to get across both to the insurgent and to the population, particularly in the rural areas which have been under insurgent domination and from which many of the insurgent recruits will have come.

There are many points with regard to treatment of surrendered personnel that need to be carefully watched. All government forces must be given the strictest orders on how to treat those who surrender and those who are captured. Any breach of these orders must be punished with the sternest disciplinary measures. Surrendered personnel should be kept completely separate from those who have been captured or arrested. It is most important to remember that at this point the insurgent who has surrendered has broken with a way of life which he had previously been prepared to accept. He lacks both faith and confidence, and his state of mind is in a vacuum. He should therefore be kept occupied as a form of therapy. He should not be just imprisoned and allowed to brood, otherwise he will merely convince himself that he made a mistake in surrendering.

In order to adopt the right treatment it will be necessary, after interrogation and processing, to divide surrendered personnel into a number of categories:

(*a*) Those who are harmless, are of no further use to the government and can safely be allowed to rejoin their families immediately.

(*b*) Those who are of further use to the government, either in intelligence or in propaganda work, and who can be given such employment with the government.

(*c*) Those who are harmless and of no further use to the government, but who either have no employment or whose families are unable to support them. These should be sent either to a local rehabilitation camp, or to a specially selected village where they can be given further education, taught a trade or usefully employed. These camps and villages should be sited in a safe area, and the surrendered personnel should preferably be unguarded other than by themselves. (The 'unguarded' is important because the risk of one backslider is well worth the feeling of faith and confidence in the government which is built up in the remainder.)

(*d*) Those who may have to stand trial for their crimes. In fact, no one should be prosecuted because it is most unlikely that the more brutal types will surrender. However, there may be borderline cases which require continued detention for at least a period. They should be sent to a special rehabilitation camp (unless satisfactory local facilities can be provided) where there are facilities for education and learning a trade, but the camp should be guarded. They should be eligible for promotion to (c).

It is most important that, whether an individual insurgent surrenders or is captured, he should be given good treatment by his immediate captors. The question of torture has already been dealt with, but there is more to it than that. I regard it as a fundamental mistake to try to stimulate in the government forces a hate campaign towards the insurgent generally. This is dangerous for three reasons. First, it leads to ill-treatment by the armed forces of captured insurgents and suspects, and encourages bullying of the population in insurgent-controlled areas. This is degrading to the troops themselves and is bad for their morale and discipline. It also creates a completely wrong impression of the government which they represent. Second, those who are hated become too scared to surrender to their haters, even when cornered and wounded in battle. It takes a long time to build up in the minds of people subject to daily communist indoctrination and propaganda that they will be well treated if they surrender, and any case in which a person is not well treated is liable to do irreparable harm to the reputation of the government. (Just think what a superb line it is if the government can say and get across to the insurgent: 'Leave your wounded behind after a battle: we will look after them'.) Third, if the government is going to win, it is going to have to live with the after-effects. If there is a hate campaign, which will involve more than just the insurgents because it will include their relatives, supporters and others who live in insurgent-dominated areas, the government will find it very difficult to bring these persons back into the body politic as loyal and useful citizens ready to play their part in the future progress of the country. The sooner wounds can be healed the better.

There are many other aspects of psychological warfare, and the intelligence organization can provide many facts and incidents which can be exploited locally to sow discord in the insurgent ranks or between the insurgents and the population. The enemy will be guilty of many mistakes and human errors. The predilection of some insurgent leaders for either brandy or girls can provide plenty of scope for psychological warfare experts and artists. One political commissar in Malaya made, and meant, the unfortunate remark: 'The only way to liberate women is to loosen their trouser belts!' Subsequent attempts to exploit and illustrate this in leaflet form were considered unsuitable for publication.

In conventional war between two countries there is no question but that psychological warfare directed at enemy units is mainly a military responsibility. In an insurgency, however, it is an internal political matter and should be a civilian responsibility, particularly in respect of its planning and production. The military, however, have an important role in its distribution through the media of voice aircraft and leaflet drops, whether by air or by armed patrols. The best distribution medium, because it is indirect and therefore subtle, is to route the message through the population with which the insurgent is in contact. For example, the use of a surrendered insurgent for propaganda work in the villages where he operated is a most convincing method of getting across the government's message. All stories improve in the retelling and the final insurgent hearer is more likely to accept the truth through a non-government channel.

The best organizational arrangement is probably for the psychological warfare section to be in the position of an independent subsidiary to the information services as a whole but working in close liaison, so that under no circumstances is there any contradiction in what is put out by each of them. The information services, which have their normal function quite outside the insurgency, should still be the government's main instrument in handling the whole of its public relations and publicity towards the population. These services are responsible for putting across all that the government is trying to do in accordance with its policies (discussed in Chapter 5). The services are responsible for publishing and making known all new laws and regulations and the reasons for them, and for giving publicity to the government's achievements in the material field. If these achievements are successful and produce results, then the information services' task is comparatively simple; but they cannot make bricks without straw. The guide is the formula mentioned in Chapter 5, which should prompt the information services to emphasize the government's legality, construction and results in juxtaposition with the insurgents' illegality, destruction and promises. By adopting a dynamic approach to the government's achievements and intentions, the information services can obtain and hold the initiative against insurgent propaganda.

If the function of information is to inform, that of propaganda is to persuade. In order to persuade people of something, it is necessary that it should be believed. There are certain guiding principles on which the information services should work. The most precious propaganda asset of the government is its credit in the eyes of the people. That credit can only be preserved by strict adherence to the truth. This is a practical consideration, not merely a moral one: one government information officer who prevaricates with the truth will, if the truth subsequently becomes apparent, undo the good work of hundreds of other officers, because the very simplest peasant is capable of drawing the conclusion that the government which such an officer represents lacks faith in its own cause. Propaganda must not be allowed to grow into an object for its own sake: gilding the lily is worse than superfluous, it is actually harmful, for truth made to sound too glowing is no longer believed. An understatement is therefore better than an overstatement. Factual information is the source of the most effective themes for propaganda, and, above all, care should be taken to appeal to sections of the population with facts that concern them directly. On the other hand, the regular vehicles of publicity, like magazines, photo-posters and radio programmes, can only hope to win and hold their audience by being interesting and entertaining as well as informative.

Polemics and direct argument with the enemy are dangerous for a number of reasons. They give the enemy the propaganda initiative and inevitably give wider circulation to the enemy's arguments. It is hard to disengage when one wants to without giving the other side the last word. There is a tendency to be drawn away from essentials and on to ground more favourable to the enemy. There is a temptation to make rash statements or rash promises. Worst of all, the people are

placed in the position of a neutral audience for whose attention
two equal parties are contending, instead of it being taken for
granted that people and government are one and indivisible
against the insurgent.

To summarize, it is vital that the government should gain
the propaganda initiative by developing its own themes based
on practical policy, thereby forcing the insurgent to try and
counter the government's arguments based on its achievements.

What counts most in propaganda as in publicity is often
much less the detail of what is said than the impression left on
the hearer's or reader's mind. For this reason any temptation
to outdo the communists at their own methods on their own
themes should be resisted. Communist propaganda is less
effective than it is given credit for, and in many cases would
be lost on the people altogether if it were not backed up by
terrorism. Moreover, communism itself is normally alien to
the people and their traditions (for which reason the communists do not plug it), and therefore all who are concerned
with information work must emphasize the contrast with
communism of the government's cause by being different in
method and approach as well as in ideas. The impression left
on the peasant by the difference of method and approach will
be quite as great as the impression left by the ideas themselves.
The tone of the government's publications must above all
reflect confidence, and care must be taken to avoid an
apologetic or defensive tone. As the constituted authority in
the country, the government should enjoy the respect of the
people, and its utterances must therefore be dignified and bear
an authoritative ring. If mistakes are made, and there will be
plenty, the information services cannot be expected to justify
them. Emphasis should be placed instead on the corrective
measures taken, or the compensation paid, thereby helping to
play down the original error, which should never be concealed
or denied.

In the organization of the information services, priority
should be given to the planning and production side of the
various sections. The distribution side, which is largely a
matter of hardware, presents fewer difficulties. Too much

attention in Vietnam was paid to the hardware, and there was never any shortage of film projectors, mobile information units and radio transmitters. But it is a complete fallacy to assume that, because one radio station fails to put the message across, therefore six regional stations are needed and, if those fail, twenty-five provincial stations. It will not be long before someone advocates and provides television. It is in the planning and production side that the main effort is required, and it is this for which professionals need to be trained. Without good directors, editors and cutters, dozens of cameramen merely produce millions of feet of useless film. Timing is also of the essence, and it is important that the information services should have very close liaison with all government departments, including the armed forces, so that their resources can be directed to publicizing the policy that is currently important. Too often the public only gets a weak explanation days after the event.

Of all the media under government control, short documentary films are probably the best in a rural agricultural community, particularly if the audience is attracted by ordinary entertainment films ('Tarzan' was a winner in Malaya). But the most important medium of all, not under government control, is the press.

In time of war, with so many lives at stake, not to mention the national interest, most governments take powers to control the press, normally through censorship. In an insurgency, when as the result of subversion certain sections of the press may have been penetrated, it would not be unreasonable for a government to take similar powers. Moreover, in the critical periods of an insurgency, when rumours are rife and tensions high between different sections of the community, the situation can easily be aggravated by irresponsible or biased reporting. In spite of this, however, it is my view that censorship should be avoided because a free press, which though sometimes critical is mainly on the side of the government, is one of the most powerful weapons in the whole armoury of the government. I remember visiting one of the best province chiefs in Vietnam in 1964, who, during his briefing, listed among the requirements for victory a 'free press'. When asked what he meant by this, he replied: 'One that is 50 per cent on the side of the government instead of 95 per cent against!'

We all understood exactly what he meant. During the period after the fall of President Diem, newspapers in Saigon sprang up overnight like toadstools. Whereas Japan has eight national dailies, and Malaya, where four languages have to be catered for, less than ten, Saigon was well on the way to producing a hundred. This press thrived on rumours and malicious gossip and depended to a large extent for its funds on blackmail. No one was safe from a smear campaign. If censorship is not to be imposed in such circumstances, some measure of control must be exercised so that daily newspapers are established which can perform a useful and responsible function.

The first answer is that a daily newspaper must be a straight-forward commercial proposition, depending for income on sales and advertisements without reliance on any form of subsidy such as cheap newsprint. To secure this, a registration system may be necessary under which the registrar has powers to enquire into the background of those responsible for the paper to ensure that there is substantial financial support for it. There are other conditions which can also be laid down. If such conditions are not met, registration should be refused. The control mechanism of registration and the sanction of suspension by the registrar should preferably not be exercised through the Ministry of Information but through either the Ministry of the Interior or the Prime Minister's Office. On the positive side, it is the Ministry of Information which should be responsible for providing the press with all facilities for gathering news from government and other sources. This is important in a country where newspapers do not have, and probably cannot afford to have, country-wide reporter cover-age. A daily issue of news stories, with facilities for any reporter to follow them up, is also greatly to be preferred to frequent press conferences, which should only be used as a means of putting across a major change in government policies.

It goes without saying that at a time of insurgency the government should make it quite clear that any breach of confidence or any security leak will be severely dealt with by at least withdrawal of facilities or even suspension of the newspaper concerned. This is well understood by most reporters, even though it may mean suppression of a scoop. There was a case in Malaya when a well-known reporter got wind of the fact that Hor Lung, the leading terrorist in Johore and second-in-command for the whole country, had surrendered. When he sought confirmation, he was rushed to the highest level and informed that it was true but that under no circumstances must it be published, possibly for months, since highly delicate operations were being conducted to use Hor Lung to secure the surrender of all the remaining units which had operated under his command in Johore. These would have been completely jeopardized if knowledge of Hor Lung's surrender to the government had reached the units. The reporter respected the confidence and had to wait several months, but he got his scoop in the end.

The foreign press presents a different problem, particularly that element which represents the country of a major power supporting the government. At the end of 1962, long before the Buddhist troubles, President Diem said to me on one occasion: 'This war can only be lost by the American press'. There was a degree of truth in this remark, though he would not have recognized that he and his family were major contributors to the row which later developed. He could not be persuaded that the only answer to foreign press criticism is to ignore it completely, to get on with the job and to let events speak for themselves. It was not the answer to allow persons like Madame Ngo Dinh Nhu (the President's sister-in-law) to fan small flames into big fires which merely obscured the real issues.

Criticism of the local government and its leading personalities is the most controversial field in which the foreign press reporter can become involved. There will be a tendency to crusade, and to expect, or even demand, a performance and standard from the local government which does not obtain in the country of the foreign press itself. It should not be surprising if such criticism is resented and leads to the expulsion of the journalist concerned (as already stated, it would be better

to ignore him, but that is asking a lot of human nature).
There will also be an emphasis on mistakes, failures and short-
comings, which always have a greater news value than things
that go right. How often does a telephone enquiry from a
reporter end: 'Well, thanks a lot. Give me a ring if anything
goes wrong!' It is, after all, easy to censure; but fair and
constructive criticism is not so easy, which is why it is so seldom
practised. It is also dull.

A foreign press reporter may regard his duty to the public
of his own country as paramount, but if his criticism is
designed to influence events in the country in which he is
enjoying a temporary assignment, he must be prepared to
accept some responsibility for its effects. The inhabitants of the
country have to face the consequences even if he does not.

Criticism by a reporter of his own government's policies and
actions, all perfectly proper and natural in the home environment, can well be misconstrued locally as indicating a lack of
confidence in those policies and a loss of resolution by the
government of the supporting power. If the foreign press is
perceptive, in spite of all the attention that may be paid to
day-to-day operations or lavished on criticism, it will appreciate that, as in all forms of human contest, an insurgency is a
test of stamina and will. The chief role of the foreign press will
be to condition its own people, which in turn will have its local
effect, to a long-drawn-out struggle which can only be won by
patience, determination and resolution.

If such perception is to be obtained, and there were many
reporters in Vietnam who made every effort, it is not enough
merely to provide the foreign press with 'facilities'. This will
only result in the main reporting interest being centred on
operations and incidents in which the reporter's own nationals
are involved, or else on spectacular or sensational incidents,
all of which are a poor guide to the general conduct or progress
of the campaign. This particularly applies when these incidents
are publicized in isolation from the slow, routine, methodical
measures required to defeat an insurgency. There is a magnetic
attraction in large-scale helicopter operations or in the use of
napalm, for example, which magnifies their importance as a
constant in counter-insurgency warfare, while there is no

counter-balancing attention given to the constructive and beneficial measures which are the main feature of the campaign and of foreign aid. It is no wonder that Hanoi could draw for so much of its propaganda on excerpts from the American press.

The remedy can lie only in guidance from the very top level of those engaged in the campaign, with more off-the-record briefings on the general strategy and less quotable interviews on daily events. The latter can be delegated, whereas the former cannot. An understanding and sympathetic press, particularly in adversity, is one of a commander's greatest assets and is worth a great deal more than many other weapons in his armoury.

Chapter 9

Balance of Forces

IN Malaya there were basically two government forces: the armed forces and the police. Their approximate strengths have already been mentioned, and it should be noted that the strength of the police force was more than twice that of the armed forces, including the Commonwealth battalions. There was a third organization, the Home Guard, which operated under police control although it was separately recruited and administered. The original police strength at the outbreak of the Emergency was 11,285 all ranks. This was built up to nearly 30,000 regulars plus over 30,000 special constables. The latter were used mainly in a defensive role in villages and on estates and mines. As part of the police force there was also established a field force composed of platoons and companies equivalent to very light infantry. The police were therefore able to carry out their normal functions, to provide protection and to undertake semi-military operations requiring units up to company strength. The armed forces acted in support of the civil power, and this, coupled with the dominance of the police force, resulted in political stability and the continuance of the rule of law throughout the insurgency.

In Vietnam there were approximately eight organizations: the armed forces, the Civil Guard, the Self-Defence Corps, the Gendarmerie, the National Police, the special forces, the Republican Youth and the Hamlet Militia, not to mention Madame Nhu's Women's Solidarity Movement. It is not easy to compare their roles with the equivalent forces in Malaya, but, excluding the armed forces and the police, they approximated roughly as follows: the Civil Guard were equivalent to the police field force, the Self-Defence Corps to the special constabulary, and the Republican Youth and Hamlet Militia to the Home Guard. The main function of the Gendarmerie (a small force of 1,200) was to arrest the military for civil offences, normally traffic accidents. Obviously, such a collection of forces was bound to lead to confusion over roles and tasks, and the co-ordination of their effort alone was an insuperable problem. There would have been much greater prospects of success if many of these forces had been amalgamated and their roles rationalized. As it was, the size and ubiquity of the army, coupled with this conglomeration of para-military forces, led to a state of political instability and a situation in which the rule of force rather than the rule of law prevailed.

In considering the government's force requirements in an insurgency, one must take into account both the insurgents' organization and the type of area in which the government has to operate, including problems of terrain. At the outset of open insurgency there are three main areas of activity. First there is the populated area under government control, including the main towns. Here the insurgent threat is subversion, minor terrorist acts, sabotage and propaganda. Eliminating this threat is obviously the responsibility of the police, assisted by the intelligence organization. In order to maintain security within the area, additional police may be required in the towns, while in the villages it should be possible to organize the first units of a home guard (or hamlet militia) organization. The only responsibility of the armed forces is the protection of their own installations.

The second is the rural populated area where control is disputed between the government and the insurgents. Here the threat is dual: in addition to subversion, terrorist acts, sabotage and propaganda, there will be village guerilla squads directly supporting the subversion, themselves supported in turn by district or regional insurgent units from platoon to company strength. This area should also be mainly a police responsibility, but military support will be required to clear it of insurgent units sector by sector in accordance with planned priorities.

The third is the remoter lightly populated area, including jungles and swamps, which is under insurgent control. Here the threat will be the same as in the first two areas but will include insurgent regular units as they are built up. This area should be entirely a military responsibility, with some assistance being given by the intelligence organization, but, in accordance with the basic principles of counter-insurgency, it should be accorded the lowest priority in the initial stages of the insurgency.

Viewed in this way, it becomes apparent that the government's immediate need is to expand its police force, including the intelligence organization. This need not be a crash programme, because all experience in the past has shown that an insurgency takes quite a time to gather momentum. Additional fully trained regular police will be required to maintain law and order, to provide security in the towns and to form a reserve for taking over disputed areas as they are brought under government control. An armed constabulary, not fully trained as regular police constables, will also be required to provide close defence of essential installations and vital points, including rural police stations. And, finally, a police field force with units up to company strength will need to be formed to operate in the disputed area, where the government is attempting to regain control in accordance with its overall plan.

If there is an army of reasonable size which has been conventionally trained and organized for the defence of the country, its immediate requirement is not expansion but retraining, with some re-organization for its counter-insurgency roles. Its priority role is to support the government programme for regaining control in the disputed areas. In the early stages this requires that the army should be able to operate in units of platoon to company size, though there may be a few occasions when battalion operations are necessary. This role can best be described as that of establishing, or re-establishing, the government's security framework in the disputed rural areas. The army's secondary role is to penetrate the insurgent-controlled areas in order to keep the insurgent units off balance and if possible dispersed. At the same time, by deep jungle penetration techniques, it should attempt to deny the insurgents freedom of movement within their own areas. In both these roles the requirement is a highly trained and disciplined professional army, not a massive popular army. (Some of the arguments against a large army have already been given in the second half of Chapter 4.)

The really difficult operations are those which have to be conducted in the populated disputed areas. The army's role here is to clear the main insurgent units out of the area over which the government is attempting to regain control, and to keep them out. Elimination of the units and the killing of insurgents is a secondary consideration at this stage. After clearing, it is the role of the police field force units, supported by the regular police and civilian government departments, to hold the area, restore government authority and win the people to the side of the government. If the selected area is sufficiently limited so that the government forces can saturate it, it is unlikely that the insurgents will seek a major battle. This is highly to be desired because the government forces do not want to have large firefights, employing heavy weapons and even aircraft, in the villages where they are attempting to regain control. As already mentioned, that type of action is liable to create more communists than it kills and makes the problem of pacification that much harder. So often one heard from good province chiefs in Vietnam (all military officers), particularly in 1962 when some progress was being made, that they would much prefer to have two or three extra Civil Guard companies rather than an army battalion for this type of operation. The killing battles will take place after the government has made progress in the populated areas to an extent where the insurgent units either are pushed back into the jungles and swamps, or are themselves forced to seek battle with the government forces in order to retain control over areas which they are losing. In the former case there will be a long period of mopping-up by a process of attrition, but in the latter case all the advantages should lie with the government.

The air force has an important dual role to play. The first is a transport role to provide mobility for, and flexibility in the use of, government forces on the ground. This involves all aspects, ranging from dropping parachute battalions and supplies to the evacuation of the wounded. The helicopter is one of the greatest modern assets to a government faced with insurgency. Quite apart from its value in operations for the quick movement of troops (such as the 'eagle flights' in Vietnam), it has a most useful communication role in keeping contact with outposts for inspection and supply purposes, in evacuating wounded and in reconnaissance. Its use should not, however, be overrated to such an extent that operations are considered impossible without it. It is not a substitute for feet on the ground. For example, it would have helped a lot in Vietnam if more of the helicopters used on major operations had been available for little things such as distributing monthly pay to units in outposts, many of whom were often six months in arrears. Not only was this state of affairs bad for morale, but it also meant that food was often seized from the local peasant without payment. The civilian flying-clubs in Malaya were used frequently in this role, particularly to drop the monthly wages for estates and mines whose managers wisely did not like to risk the road journey with large amounts of cash. Pay convoys on the roads in Vietnam were at one stage a frequent Viet Cong target.

The secondary role of the air force is, of course, tactical air support for the ground forces. This is a role that must be fulfilled with the very greatest discretion. It must not be used so indiscriminately that it completely alienates the peasantry in areas not controlled by the government; but, at the same time, it would be foolish not to use this powerful weapon on good targets of opportunity, for example where ground forces, having made contact with a major insurgent unit, have pinned it down and can pinpoint its exact position. The real value of the air force in this role is not so much in the casualties it may inflict on the insurgent units (which are liable to be exaggerated) as in the overall psychological effect which the threat of such an attack has on insurgent methods of operation. While the government has in its possession this powerful tactical weapon, the insurgents will be chary of concentrating their forces in any numbers, particularly in daylight in the open. Even at night, with the use of flares, villages and posts under insurgent attack can be supported, and in many instances in Vietnam the arrival of a 'flareship' alone was sufficient to break off an attack. Tactical air support is one reason, if not the most important, why the insurgents can be restricted to guerilla warfare and prevented from developing a war of movement. But it must be recognized that its too constant use will develop in the ground forces a disinclination to attack without it, and in the insurgent forces a familiarity which will enable them to counter its effectiveness.

Unavoidably the navy has a very limited role in an insurgency. There were no known attempts to infiltrate either individuals or arms into Malaya by sea. In Vietnam, however, the situation was very different, and the navy had an important part to play in patrolling the sea coast to intercept such infiltration from the North and in preventing movement of insurgent units along the coast and in the mouths of the main rivers. For this purpose the main requirement is small patrol vessels (about 100-120 feet) capable of staying at sea for a week and doing over twenty knots when required. All should be equipped with a small radar set capable of picking up sampans and other small vessels within a radius of two to five miles at night.

There is one other small type of force which may be required where there are ethnic minorities, such as aboriginal tribes, living in the jungles and mountains. This is the main, and in my view the sole, reason for the establishment of special forces: to make contact with such tribes and to recruit and organize them into units for their own defence on the side of the government. This cannot normally be done until the government has gained such control of its populated areas on the plains and in the foothills that it is ready to carry out effective deep penetration operations in the mountain jungles. The establishment in the populated areas of similar units amongst other groups of the population is not desirable because such units tend to become independent private armies, owing allegiance less to the government than to some territorial local figure, and as a result bearing little responsibility for their actions. Also, their operations in such areas tend to develop into guerilla-versus-guerilla actions, which, while successful in inflicting casualties on the insurgent, never terminate and fail to restore permanent order to the area. They merely create a never-ending situation of civil war.

Just as it is not possible to lay down any fixed ratio for the size of the government forces in relation to the insurgent, so it is impossible to give more than a rough guide to the balance of forces as between the regular armed forces and the para-military forces, whether amalgamated into one police-type organization or not. There are many factors other than operational roles which have to be taken into account, such as the capital and recurrent costs of training, equipping and maintaining a soldier, which are at least one and a half times as great as those for a policeman, even one employed in a field-force role. Terms of service and demobilization problems have to be considered. For example, the police force can offer a life career to its regulars; even a police constable can still happily patrol his beat or perform other similar duties after twenty-five years' service, and he has a pension to look forward to as well. This is not the case in an army, where ten years' service is perhaps the maximum that can be expected of a private infantry soldier. The government is then faced with the payment of gratuities and the problem of re-absorbing ex-servicemen into civilian occupations or land resettlement schemes in order to avoid, after a large-scale demobilization, the formation of a potentially dangerous pressure group of disgruntled ex-servicemen. If, on the other hand, a private soldier's career is extended beyond ten years, the platoons will begin to puff a bit when going uphill.

But for political and psychological reasons, the question of conscription is perhaps the most vital of these factors. The government's cause is immeasurably strengthened if all its forces are composed of volunteers. This should not be so difficult in countries where youth forms such a high proportion of the population, and where young men are ready, willing and able to bear arms, provided that they can expect to be well trained, well equipped and regularly paid (with reasonable pension provisions in the event of death or disability). The regular police force, because it offers a life career, should have no difficulty in attracting the highest standard of young men for country-wide service. For those recruited on a temporary basis during an insurgency, the police force can offer, more conveniently than the army, terms which enable the young man to serve in his own district or province. When reasonably secure conditions prevail in such areas, recruiting is generally no problem. This was certainly the case in Vietnam with regard to recruits for the Civil Guard and Self-Defence Corps.

The army, by contrast, can offer only temporary service on a country-wide basis and is therefore likely to be the less attractive. It was unfortunate in Vietnam that the size of the army dictated an element of conscription even though this was little more than 20 per cent of the total armed forces. This involved all the problems connected with call-up and draft-dodging and provided the Viet Cong with an effective propaganda item. Conscription was applied in Malaya for the special constabulary not because there was a shortage of volunteers amongst the Malays but in order to induce the other races to play their part. It had some surprising results. Many young Chinese took off for Singapore, where conscription did not apply, or for China, from which they were subsequently not allowed to return. This demonstration of unwillingness to serve put the Chinese community on their mettle in order to prove their loyalty. As soon as adequate recruits among the non-Malays were forthcoming, the law was dropped and the government could again claim that all its forces were composed of volunteers. It was a great pity that this was not the case in Vietnam merely because of a small percentage in the army. This could have been avoided by increasing instead the numbers of the Civil Guard, in which volunteer recruiting would have been easier. This would have been just as effective, if not more so, in the earlier stages of the insurgency. If the emphasis is placed on the creation and expansion of a large army, then the insurgency will automatically develop into a military problem, requiring not just a large army but a good one.

If all these factors are taken into account, including that of political stability, a rough guide to the desirable balance of forces which will allow them to be effective in their respective roles would be somewhere between two and two and a half policemen for every soldier.

Chapter 10

Basic Operational Concepts

IN the last five chapters I have dealt with the government, its organization and the type of forces required to deal with the threat of communist subversion which develops into an insurgency. It is now necessary to consider the measures and tactics required to defeat that insurgency.

As already stated in the basic principles, the government must have an overall plan to co-ordinate all military and civil effort and to lay down priorities. The plan must also take into account the fourth and fifth principles that the main emphasis should be given to defeating subversion, not the guerillas, and that the government must secure its base areas first. When applying this to action and operations on the ground, there will be four definite stages which can be summed up as clearing, holding, winning and won.

The first stage of clearing may not be necessary in the initial priority areas if they are reasonably secure, but, in order to maintain the sequence, it will be assumed that we are dealing with areas containing insurgent units which must be cleared before the next three stages can follow. For 'clear' operations the military tactics will vary according to the terrain and the size and composition of the insurgent units. The area itself should be selected as an extension of an area already securely held, and should first be subjected to an intense intelligence effort before any operations start. It helps if there are natural boundaries with a good central communication access. Having selected the area, and prepared the plan, the first essential is to saturate it with joint military and police forces. This will force the insurgent units either to disperse within the area or possibly to withdraw to neighbouring areas still under their control or disputed. The government's forces should then be so deployed as to make it impossible for the insurgent forces to reconcentrate within the area or to re-infiltrate from outside. Clear operations will, however, be a waste of time unless the government is ready to follow them up immediately with 'hold' operations. If there is no follow-up, then the clear operation will develop into no more than a general sweep through the area, which, when the government forces withdraw, will revert to its original state. This does positive harm to the government's cause (for reasons already explained) and psychologically suggests to the people that the guerilla mosquito is proof against the government sledgehammer. Sweep operations are only justified when carried out in neighbouring areas in conjunction with a nearby clear operation in order to prevent insurgent reinforcements entering the area of the clear operation, and to keep the insurgents off balance while the clear and subsequent hold operations are being carried out.

The measures required in 'hold' operations will vary according to whether the area was originally comparatively secure, with a minimum of clearing therefore required, or whether it was disputed territory subject first to a clear operation. The objects of a hold operation are to restore government authority in the area and to establish a firm security framework. This involves the creation of strategic hamlets, the formation of hamlet militia and the imposition of various control measures on the movement of both people and resources, all of which are designed to isolate the guerilla forces from the population, to provide protection for the people themselves and to eliminate the insurgent underground subversive organization in the villages. This hold period of operations inevitably takes a considerable time and requires a methodical approach and a great attention to detail. It never really ends, and it certainly overlaps into the following stage of 'winning' the population over to positive support of the government.

'Winning' the population can tritely be summed up as good government in all its aspects. From the point of view of the immediate impact, there are many minor social benefits which can easily and fairly inexpensively be provided, such as improved health measures and clinics (it is a fact that no population suffering from debilitating diseases will ever take positive action either on behalf of the government or even on its own behalf); new schools (education for their children is

Doesn't mention destroying villages and then trying to resettle the people.

probably the priority demand in most rural communities); and improved livelihood and standard of living. This last point covers every aspect of increased agricultural production, including better seeds, livestock and poultry, and the provision of fruit trees and other suitable cash crops. More desirable than outright gifts are schemes which are self-perpetuating or encourage a chain reaction. For example, building plans should stimulate the production of local building material. Improved communications are particularly important in the remoter areas, and this calls for a major programme for the repair of rural roads, canals and bridges. All this helps to give the impression not only that the government is operating for the benefit of the people but that it is carrying out programmes of a permanent nature and therefore intends to stay in the area. [This gives the people a stake in stability and hope for the future,] which in turn encourages them to take the necessary positive action to prevent insurgent reinfiltration and to provide the intelligence necessary to eradicate any insurgent cells which remain.

When normal conditions have been restored, and the people have demonstrated by their positive action that they are on the side of the government, then, as soon as the government advance has been extended well beyond the area so that the threat of insurgent reinfiltration is removed, the area can be declared 'white'. The government has 'won'. All restrictions can be removed, and greater attention can be given to the government's long-term aim of creating a politically and economically stable and viable community. The seeds of democracy planted during the winning stage can now begin to sprout. Economically this is the time when more ambitious self-help projects become feasible, and, in the urban areas, secondary industry will begin to grow and flourish of its own accord. It is a great mistake to imagine that either democracy or economic progress can be forced in unstable conditions. They will achieve a far more dynamic growth when normal conditions are restored and the population's energies, relieved from the strain of war, can be released for constructive purposes.

These four phases are simple enough to understand in the

areas where government operations can be started and to which its limited resources can be applied. The really difficult problem lies in the non-priority areas, where the government must hold out and prevent the insurgents from gaining full control. A very careful assessment is required of the insurgent potential in these areas as compared with the remaining resources available to the government. Depending on this, the government must then decide whether to let a few outlying areas go and to ignore them until such time as the whole programme has advanced sufficiently for further resources to be made available. This is a difficult decision for a government to take, and there is always a risk that such areas, however unimportant, may be declared 'liberated' by the insurgents. This may have to be accepted, provided that the government, by using its reserve forces during a period of lull in the priority areas, can undertake operations in such areas with the object of showing the flag. This type of operation requires very careful handling indeed; under no circumstances must it be carried out as a punitive raid into enemy territory. Its purpose is psychological rather than military, and it is designed to show the population still living there that the government has not forgotten them and that it will return as soon as it is in a position to do so. The intention of the operation is to encourage the people to welcome the future return of the government, not, as was so frequently the case in Vietnam, to make them hope that the government forces never show their faces in the area again.

Apart from these areas, which become to all intents and purposes insurgent-controlled, there will be a considerable area of disputed territory in provinces which are of a low priority. Here the aim of the government must be to keep its flag flying in the main centres of population, such as the province capitals and district towns, and to accept that, outside these, what the government controls by day may be controlled by the insurgents by night. In these circumstances no effort should be made to involve the inhabitants on the side of the government: it is merely asking them to commit suicide. No attempts should be made to conduct clear operations by forces operating through the villages and hamlets of such areas when

there is no prospect of holding any area which may be cleared.] ☆
The main purposes of operations and patrols are to keep
insurgent forces on the move, to lay ambushes at likely points
and to obtain tactical information, i.e. to keep the areas disputed and to prevent them from falling fully under insurgent
control.

It must be recognized that the insurgents require control
only for limited purposes: to obtain supplies, recruits and
intelligence and to prevent the inhabitants of the area giving
the government any positive support. They are not at this
stage attempting to establish an elaborate rival administration
or government, though they may carry out some land redis-
tribution and will certainly collect taxes. It is therefore
important to keep offensive operations going in the disputed
areas to thwart the insurgents' purpose—for example, with the
aim of buying up all surplus rice stocks. If possible, such
operations should be combined with a very limited strategic
hamlet programme in the immediate vicinity of district towns
and province capitals. This will provide experience and a
firmer base from which clear-and-hold operations can be
started when the area is accorded a greater priority. The
offensive spirit must be maintained, and any tendency just to
fall back on the static defence of district towns and other vital
points must be avoided. This situation requires the best
officers and the most disciplined troops because it is the hardest
task of all to play a waiting game.

* * *

As for the more military aspect of operations, a number of
books have already been written on tactics and personal
experience in guerilla warfare, and there have been further
developments in Vietnam which are bound to be the subject
of more books. I have only one general point to make, which
I call the 'Same-Element Theory of Guerilla Warfare'.

It is the secret of guerilla forces that, to be successful, they
must hold the initiative, attack selected targets at a time of
their own choosing and avoid battle when the odds are against
them. If they can maintain their offensive in this way, both

their strength and their morale automatically increase until victory is won. As a corollary, it must be the aim of counter-guerilla forces to compel guerilla forces to go on the defensive so that they lose the initiative, become dispersed and expend their energy on mere existence. Their condition then changes from one of automatic expansion to one of certain contraction, as a result of which both their strength and their morale steadily decline.

The aim of the government's forces must therefore be to force the insurgent to go on the defensive. In order to achieve this, in addition to maintaining a high rate of operations and continually improving the contact rate, the basic principle which should govern military strategy and tactics must be to engage the guerilla forces in their own element. There are three such elements: the populated areas, including the popular bases of the insurgents, from which they draw their main support; the unpopulated areas or war zones, which provide sanctuary and training areas for their main forces; and their communications, particularly those between the popular bases and the war zones.

The battle in the populated areas represents a straight fight between the government and the insurgents for the control of the rural population. The main method required to restore government authority and control is the strategic hamlet programme, supported by 'clear-and-hold' operations. The purpose of the programme, supported by these operations, is not just to kill insurgents in the populated areas but to destroy the insurgent subversive organization and infrastructure there. The mere killing of insurgents, without the simultaneous destruction of their infrastructure, is a waste of effort because their subversive organization will continue to spread and all casualties will be made good by new recruits.

The strategic hamlet programme, properly implemented and supported by clear-and-hold operations, will gradually destroy the insurgent infrastructure. This has two simultaneous effects: first, it forces the insurgent units to fight to preserve their infrastructure at the point at which government forces are at their most concentrated and strongest, thereby automatically increasing the contact-and-kill rate; and, second,

Must fight guerilla at their own game.

it reduces their sources of supplies and new recruits. The reason for the success which will be gained from this type of operation is that the government forces are fighting in the same element and for the same purpose (control of the population) as the insurgent forces to which they are opposed.

The chief emphasis, therefore, must be on 'clear-and-hold' operations as opposed to 'search-and-clear' operations (or sweeps). Search-and-clear operations, however aggressive, do not achieve the dual purpose of killing insurgents and destroying their infrastructure. The ratio of contacts and the number of insurgents killed are very limited and depend greatly on chance. Moreover, this type of operation often requires the most tremendous effort by large-scale air and ground forces, which is wasteful. The reason for its lack of success is that it does not put the government forces into the same element as the insurgent forces opposed to them. As a result, it does not force insurgent units to fight in defence of their organization and infrastructure, because it does not threaten these at all.

The unpopulated areas are the war zones of the insurgents, where their main forces can be trained and grouped for offensive operations in support of their own programme for gaining control of the populated areas of the country. The principle here is exactly the same as in the populated areas. The government forces must operate in these areas under similar conditions to the insurgent. This requires that regular military units, not only companies of the Ranger type, must be trained for long-term deep penetration operations, particularly in mountain and jungle. Short-term raids into the war zones, no matter how offensive or large their scale, achieve no lasting results. Some insurgents may be killed, some dumps may be found, but within a short time all such losses are made good.

The secret of the insurgents' strength in these areas is their freedom of movement, allowing them to concentrate or disperse their forces at will. The type of operation required is one in which government forces are inserted into the area as covertly as possible and maintained there for a long period, by air supply if necessary (there are a number of techniques whereby air supply need not give away their position).

Units should be confined to comparatively restricted areas so that their own movement, which makes them vulnerable, is limited, and so that they can maintain almost permanent ambushes on tracks which the insurgents must use. Not only will this inflict casualties on the insurgents, but it will deny them freedom of movement and gradually break down their essential communication and supply systems. This in turn causes their units to disperse into small parties and forces them to seek food and other supplies on the perimeter of the populated areas, where they are even more vulnerable to small ambushes. Again it will be seen that the more government forces can operate in exactly the same element as the insurgent, the greater will be their success.

The type of operations just described will also be effective against insurgent communications within their war zones in the mountain and jungle areas of the country. Similar operations on a smaller scale and for shorter periods, carried out both by military and by para-military forces on the perimeter of the populated areas (within one to five hours patrolling time), will, by using ambushes as a main tactic, disrupt the insurgent communications between the populated areas and their war zones.

It is not often realized that in guerilla warfare guerilla forces are just as vulnerable to ambushes as are government forces. One reads so often of government convoys being ambushed on main roads, or of government forces being ambushed on their way to give relief to a post under attack (a favourite Viet Cong tactic in Vietnam). The insurgent is just as vulnerable, particularly to small-scale ambushes. There is constant insurgent movement of forces, supplies, couriers, agents and the like. The pattern of this movement on the ground is like a spider's web, and if the intelligence effort is directed on it, many possible targets can be selected which will disrupt the insurgent supply organization and deny continued freedom of movement. Many of the most successful ambushes in Malaya were carried out by small parties of two to five men at night, on small tracks which the terrorists were known to be using. The fire power of a small party with modern weapons is such that it can safely take on a larger insurgent unit, inflict heavy casualties and then, if necessary, fade away.

In the Mekong Delta in Vietnam much greater control needed to be established over the waterways. These were the main Viet Cong communications in the Delta, as contrasted to the government's dependence on air and road. In order to get into the same element as the Viet Cong, the government itself should have made greater use of the waterways for its own requirements and, at the same time, controlled the movement of other traffic on the waterways. Control points, curfews and registration of boats were some of the measures required to give effect to this.

All this does not mean that there should be no other types of operations. When good intelligence is limited, sweep-and-clear operations in insurgent-controlled territory may be necessary to keep the insurgent forces stirred up and off balance. Such operations can have only the limited aim of killing insurgents contacted, and trying to prevent them concentrating for their own offensive operations. When intelligence improves (or as a result of another operation or insurgent attack) and an insurgent unit can be definitely located, then 'fix-and-destroy' operations are required. It must be borne in mind, however, that these operations serve only the limited purpose of killing insurgents. They do not destroy their organization or infrastructure. They must, therefore, be regarded as secondary to those operations which are achieving the primary aim.

The basic military strategy, therefore, must be to insert as many as possible of the government forces, both military and para-military, into the same element as the insurgent forces to which they are opposed. If they are not so engaged, then they are being wasted. The main military tactic should be the ambush (in the populated areas, particularly at night), and the units carrying out this tactic should restrict their movements in order to avoid being ambushed themselves—like Jim Corbett with the man-eaters.

Getting government forces into the same element as the insurgent is rather like trying to deal with a tomcat in an alley. It is no good inserting a large, fierce dog. The dog may not find the tomcat; if he does, the tomcat will escape up a tree; the dog will then chase the female cats in the alley. The answer is to put in a fiercer tomcat. The two cannot fail to meet because they are both in exactly the same element and have exactly the same purpose in life. The weaker will be eliminated.

Chapter 11

Strategic Hamlets

O F all the four stages mentioned in the last chapter the 'hold' aspect of operations is undoubtedly the most crucial and the most complex, involving as it does the establishment of a solid security framework covering the whole population living in the villages and small towns of a given area. The basis of this security framework is the strategic hamlet.

The term 'village' in Vietnam is used to describe the administrative unit below the district level, and each village contains a number of hamlets varying from two to ten. The average village has a population of about 5,000, divided into five hamlets of about 1,000 people each. These hamlets are roughly equivalent to the Malay *kampong* or Chinese village in Malaya, each again of about 1,000 inhabitants linked together in a *mukim*, which was the administrative unit next below the district. A distinction must also be drawn between a strategic hamlet (*ap-chien-luoc*) and a defended hamlet (*ap-chien-dau*) in Vietnam. The former represented a fairly scattered hamlet, with possibly some regrouping of houses, whereas the latter represented a compact hamlet, with houses grouped closely together and surrounded by a strong perimeter fence. Strategic hamlets might also be surrounded by a light fence, but this fence was symbolic and only served a minor purpose from the defence point of view. The distinction in Malaya was very much the same, where the Malay *kampongs*, with hardly any regrouping of houses, were organized for their own defence in the same way as strategic hamlets, and where the 'new villages', mainly Chinese, were regrouped and often re-sited in compact form to provide closer defence as in the case of defended hamlets.

In Malaya the failure of the mainly Chinese insurgent movement to penetrate the Malay population meant that little more was required in Malay *kampongs* than the organization of home guard units supported by police stations in key localities. This meant that the government could devote its attention to the resettlement of the Chinese squatters into new villages, of which about 600 were established before the Emergency ended, involving the movement of over half a million people. In Vietnam, by contrast, the insurgent movement had infected all areas of the countryside, which meant that strategic hamlets, even in the reasonably secure areas, needed more elaborate organization for their defence than Malay *kampongs*, and, in the bad areas, the defended hamlets required a considerable defensive organization, more so than in the new villages in Malaya, in order to provide protection.

When the strategic hamlet programme was started in Vietnam at the beginning of 1962 (although some good work in this direction had already been done in a few provinces during the previous two years), it was estimated that about 11,000 strategic and defended hamlets would be required, of which about 50 per cent would require only minor regrouping, i.e. the relocation of only a few scattered houses nearer to the centre of the hamlet; that about 30 per cent would require major regrouping, i.e. about half the houses would have to be relocated; that about 15 per cent would have to be completely regrouped, i.e. considerably more than half of the houses would have to be relocated; and that the remaining 5 per cent might have to be moved to completely new sites. In all the first three cases it was not the intention that any householder should be relocated more than a reasonable distance from his land, i.e. up to a maximum of three miles. Only in the remaining 5 per cent was it likely to be necessary to move all houses entirely to a new site, a measure that would entail loss of existing land. These last hamlets, of course, would be in the worst areas, completely under Viet Cong control, mainly close to jungles and swamps or in remote valleys. The percentages were not unreasonable at the time they were forecast, the point to remember being that if the situation improved, less relocation would have to be done, but if the situation deteriorated, then a greater relocation would have to be done. The degree of relocation therefore required in any area depends on the security situation at the time when the hold operation starts in the area.

The compact defended village is by no means a new concept in Asia. In many rural areas, particularly frontier and mountain regions, the defended village has existed for centuries as a means of protection against border raiders, local bandits and even man-eating tigers. Generally, it has been in the more heavily populated coastal plains and newly developed areas during the period of colonial law and order that the concept has died out, because it was no longer necessary. (As a Burmese village headman remarked in 1942, when asked whether he was not glad to see the colonialists being driven out by the Japanese: 'You slept in peace under the British!') In Malaya, which was of very recent development, the defended village was almost unknown except for a few forts along the coast. The same applied to the Cochinchinese area of South Vietnam, where the main development occurred during the period of French rule. In the central provinces of Annam, however, the defended village was a well-understood concept from earlier days. Descriptions by early travellers, on their arrival on the Annamite coast, of the villages which they visited might have been descriptions of well-defended strategic hamlets. The establishment of strategic and defended hamlets as one of the measures of defeating a communist insurgency has only meant that the lessons of the past have had to be relearnt.

The fundamental aim behind the establishment of the security framework based on strategic hamlets is to isolate the insurgent both physically and politically from the population. Only when this isolation is effected will successful operations against the guerilla units achieve a lasting result, because casualties can no longer be replaced by new recruits, and units have to disperse in order to exist. I put this to President Diem in the following terms:

It is most important that province chiefs and the responsible military commanders should fully understand the concept which lies behind successful anti-communist guerilla operations, i.e. the physical and political separation of the guerillas from the population. One must get all the 'little fishes' out of the 'water' and keep them out; then they die. All the required measures stem from this main aim, and in carrying out such measures, all officers must bear constantly in mind how far the measures and the manner in which they are carried out are achieving the right results. It is necessary to maintain not only the momentum (of the strategic hamlet programme) but also the aim.

The establishment of strategic hamlets has three main objects. The first, a prerequisite for the other two, is the protection of the population. This is not simply a matter of regrouping some outlying houses in the centre of the hamlet and then building a massive rampart round it of barbed wire, stakes, moats and booby traps—the sort of defence measure which was a prominent feature of many strategic and defended hamlets in Vietnam. It requires, also, preferably simultaneously, the establishment of a good radio network between hamlets, villages and the district capital, and the training and arming of men from the hamlet as hamlet militia to provide the close defence of the hamlet itself. While all this is being created during the hold phase of operations, the close defence of the hamlet must be provided by the para-military forces, with the army holding the ring to prevent attacks by major insurgent units. Both the para-military forces and the army should be so deployed at this stage that they can rescue hamlets if attacked by more than local village guerilla squads, which the hamlet militia should be capable of keeping at bay. The most vital aspect of protection, however, is the elimination within the hamlet of the insurgent underground organization. Until this is done, no hamlet will be secure against re-penetration and treachery, nor can the people themselves be expected to take positive action on behalf of the government until insurgent agents and supporters within the hamlet have been removed.

The second object of strategic hamlets is to unite the people and involve them in positive action on the side of the government. Peasants the world over are individualists, even more so when they live in scattered communities. Many would be content to live quietly in their own houses on their own land, with a few like-minded neighbouring friends and relatives, and to ignore, except for some of the necessities of life, the rest of the world. This attitude is no longer in keeping with the times nor with the general aspiration for progress and advancement. If this aspiration is to be realized, the peasant must accept that he has obligations and responsibilities to his own community. The building up of a community spirit based on common interest should follow from the creation of the strategic hamlet and its initial organization for defence. This is not all. At the same time that a local community spirit is being promoted, a sense of national solidarity must also be encouraged. This can only be done by involving the people in a small way in national policies which both affect and benefit them, first in the defence of their community and secondly in its development.

The third object of strategic hamlets is this development in the social, economic and political fields. These measures have already been mentioned under the 'winning' stage of operations: the provision of schools, clinics, markets, improved agricultural methods, water supplies, electricity, radio programmes, newspapers and improved communications, so that there is constant contact with the outside world, followed finally by local elections to village councils and national elections to a national legislature. It is at this stage that the regrouping of houses, which at first sight might have seemed a hardship, has compensating advantages. Although the man of the household may have further to go to work in his fields, his family has greater access to many amenities of life: the school is handy for the children, and the market and shops for the wife. The eventual provision of running water and electricity becomes possible in a compact community, whereas it remains financially impossible in scattered communities even in the most modern societies. Many new villages in Malaya, where all the inhabitants were resettled, looked barren and depressing when first established, but now, more than ten years later, they are thriving small towns with all modern amenities. The significant point here is that at the end of the Emergency very few families wished to leave their new homes and return to their old sites.

These three objects of the strategic hamlet programme were well understood by Ngo Dinh Nhu, the President's brother, who was mainly responsible for carrying out the programme in Vietnam. He further appreciated that if the programme was successful, it would be possible to build up on the peasant a base of political power which would more than counterbalance that of the army. In this particular respect, however, he made three mistakes: first, through the Can Lao party and the Republican Youth, he attempted to impose political control from the top instead of winning political and popular support at the bottom. Second, by putting much of the emphasis on the Republican Youth, he created seeds of conflict within the community between youth and the traditional elders. Third, he failed to comprehend the extent of Viet Cong penetration, and neither he nor his brother the President was prepared to take the necessary measures to eliminate this within the hamlets. For all the accusations of dictatorship and tyranny which were levelled at the Ngo regime, the President and his brother failed to exercise their absolute authority in the one sphere which might have saved South Vietnam.

At this point I should mention one criticism frequently levelled at the strategic-hamlet concept by military officers—that it is defensive. This shows a lack of comprehension. Certainly the first object of the programme is the protection of the population, and each hamlet must therefore be capable of defending itself. But the concept as a whole is designed to secure a firm base and then to expand from that into disputed, and finally enemy-controlled, territory. If the programme is strategically directed, and supported by the armed forces, it becomes an offensive advance which will wrest the military initiative from the insurgent. This is far more aggressive, because it is effective, than launching thousands of operations with hundreds of troops in each, all wading through the paddy fields with their rifles cocked to no purpose.

The key to the establishment of strategic and defended hamlets is detailed advance planning. During the clear stage of operations, complete surveys should be undertaken of each hamlet, and decisions made with regard to the number of houses to be moved and the number of people involved. Great care also needs to be taken with regard to the selection of sites for defended hamlets, and such factors as adequate water, access and the convenience of the site from the point of view of the inhabitants' work have to be taken into account. Defended hamlets also need to be tactically sited both for defence and as bases for offensive operations. For this reason very isolated hamlets should be avoided. Because they are expensive, defended hamlets should be established only where absolutely essential for defence purposes. Every effort should be made to avoid unnecessary movement of houses or construction work, and, as far as possible, sites within existing hamlets should be chosen where the least number of houses have to be moved. Hamlets can also be sited to serve a secondary defence purpose such as the protection of main road junctions, railway stations or even bridges.

If a careful survey has been made, then the actual movement of the people to the prepared sites can be planned as a military operation and carried out with efficiency and speed. House sites should be allocated in advance, and free transport provided so that the householder can move all his possessions. Additional building materials, especially roofing, should be available at the site so that houses can be built quickly. Householders should be given a subsidy for the purchase of such materials, and arrangements should be made for all families to be fed free for a period, until shops are opened and normal essential supplies can be obtained in the hamlet. During this period, close defence must be provided by the para-military forces until such time as a reliable hamlet militia can be raised and trained within the hamlet. If the whole operation is carefully explained to the inhabitants, and government publicity and intentions are clear, resentment at any upheaval can be kept to the minimum. It may come as a surprise to learn that, both in Vietnam and in Malaya, there were many occasions when large numbers of the population asked to be moved and did so voluntarily without any pressure being brought to bear on them. In fact it can be said that, throughout, the Vietnamese peasant understood perfectly well the whole purpose of the programme, and was prepared to play his part in carrying it out even to the extent of devoting full-time labour for the construction work involved. Only in the planting and harvesting periods was this a hardship. The

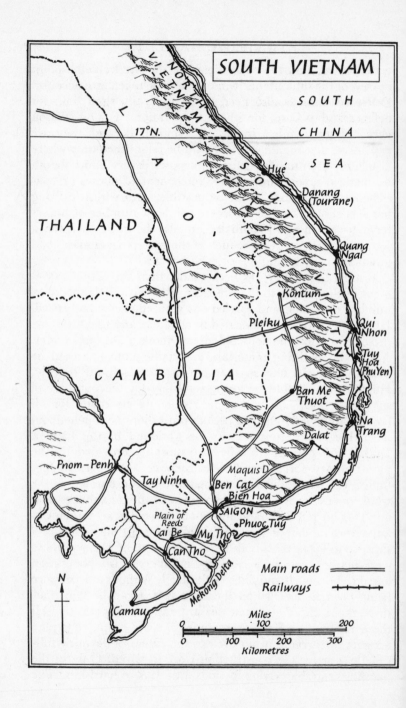

SOUTH VIETNAM

SOUTH

CHINA

SEA

NORTH VIETNAM

17°N.

THAILAND

LAOS

Hué

Danang
(Tourane)

Quang
Ngai

Kontum

Pleiku

Qui
Nhon

Tuy
Hoa
(PhuYen)

CAMBODIA

Ban Me
Thuot

Na
Trang

Dalat

Pnom-Penh

Maquis D

Tay Ninh

Ben Cat
Bien Hoa

SAIGON

Phuoc Tuy

Plain of
Reeds
Cai Be

My Tho

Can Tho

Mekong Delta

Main roads ——————

Railways ++++++++++

Camau

N

Miles
100   200

0   100   200   300
Kilometres

point that worried him was: Would it work? This raises the vital question: What went wrong with the programme in Vietnam?

As a result of impatience for action, it got off to an unfortunate start with Operation 'Sunrise' and Operation 'Sea Swallow'. With the greatly increased American aid (including helicopters at the beginning of 1962) that resulted from General Maxwell Taylor's visit at the end of 1961, there was every opportunity, because of the breathing-space which this aid provided, to get off to a good start, with a planned and well-directed campaign aimed at securing first the densely populated and well-developed vital areas of the Delta around Saigon. Instead of this, Operation 'Sunrise' was launched north of Ben Cat (thirty miles from Saigon), in one of the less populated but more heavily Viet Cong-controlled areas, with a view to establishing four defended hamlets. It involved the resettlement of all the inhabitants concerned away from their rice fields, which gave the unfortunate impression that all strategic hamlets were going to be of this type. This provided the Viet Cong with an excellent propaganda line. Considerable government forces were subsequently required to hold the hamlets, and the road to them from the province capital, running as it did through disputed territory, provided opportunities for frequent Viet Cong ambushes. These four hamlets remained hostages of fortune until they were lost to the Viet Cong in 1964. As for Operation 'Sea Swallow', which followed in Phu Yen Province, there was nothing intrinsically wrong with it except that it was not an important area and received undue priority for the limited resources which were then available. It was selected merely because the province authorities were enthusiastic to start and it was considered undesirable not to take advantage of this response. The whole operation was summed up to me by President Diem, who said: 'It makes the Americans happy, and it does not worry either me or the Viet Cong!'

Subsequently in the area round Saigon, again because of a desire to meet a local response, a start was made in hamlets of the Cao Dai sect, under the sponsorship of a local Cao Dai general, quite irrespective of where the hamlets were located (they were scattered over three provinces) and not in accordance with any overall plan.

In spite of this haphazard start in the early months of 1962, which at least provided some experience, the main programme developed well during the summer, and in September I reported to President Diem in the following terms:

Very great progress has been made over the last six months in establishing strategic hamlets throughout the provinces visited. There are, however, still some gaps both inside the hamlets, in that all the ingredients for their success have not yet been completed, and outside, in that they have not yet been established in a sufficient block to achieve a solid security framework over a wide area. If the Viet Cong reaction to them proves to be no more violent than it has been to date, there is no reason why these gaps should not be filled over the next six months and the number of strategic hamlets and the areas which they cover greatly expanded. In fact, it is most necessary to maintain the momentum of this expansion, both in order to keep the initiative and to prevent the Viet Cong planning and carrying out effective counter-measures.

There are, therefore, over the next six months, three main requirements:

(1) to improve and consolidate existing strategic hamlets so that they achieve the purpose for which they have been built;

(2) to link up existing areas of strategic hamlets so that they are mutually supporting, with no gaps in between where the population remains subject to Viet Cong penetration; and

(3) to maintain the momentum of the programme so that the area protected by strategic hamlets is steadily expanded thereby retaining the initiative and making it more difficult for the Viet Cong to disrupt the programme.

While the Viet Cong are absolutely opposed to strategic hamlets, there is no doubt that their reaction has so far been less violent than was generally expected. This is partly accounted for by the highly successful military operations that have been carried out in conjunction with the programme, but another major reason is that the strategic hamlets themselves face the Viet Cong with a dilemma. Without the people's support, the Viet Cong cannot win, but if they attack strategic hamlets, they are attacking and antagonizing the people. It is important to keep them faced with this dilemma, and there are two aspects of strategic hamlets which in some areas need to be reconsidered:

(1) I think it is a mistake to establish strong points, particularly concrete posts, outside the perimeter of strategic hamlets. Psychologically this allows the Viet Cong to attack the armed defenders without attacking the hamlet or involving the people in any way in the battle. Moreover, militarily, such posts are vulnerable to attack at night, in which case a whole section of the defence is wiped out simultaneously or at least neutralized. I much prefer the system where the main post is situated inside the hamlet, with individual camouflaged foxholes (they can be built up in an elevated position where the ground is liable to flooding) dotted around the perimeter, some close to the fence and some further back. This makes it more difficult for any attackers, because they do not know exactly where the positions are, nor whether they are all occupied or not. It is much more difficult to kill even one or two defenders dispersed in this way, and that is not enough to effect a breach in the defences.

(2) From both the psychological and the practical point of view, I think it is also a mistake to organize the evacuation of women and children from a hamlet under attack. It may look practical when rehearsed in the daytime, but at night, particularly when under fire, there must inevitably be confusion and some casualties. Furthermore, the men defending the hamlet will not know what is happening to their wives and children, and will have less incentive to defend the hamlet if there is evacuation. It would, in my view, be better if the women and children had a convenient foxhole or bunker adjacent to their houses (not inside in case of the house catching fire) where they could take shelter while the attack was going on. In the event of a hamlet being overrun, I cannot see the Viet Cong taking reprisals against the women and children even though they may burn down buildings and houses. Neighbouring hamlets, instead of receiving evacuated women and children, should be ready to provide relief and shelter for the inhabitants of a hamlet which has been overrun. If that happens, however, the key thing is to restore the hamlet, perhaps even better than it was before, as rapidly as possible. This also helps to demonstrate that the Viet Cong destroy and the government constructs.

I am a bit worried about the length of fences round some of the strategic hamlets. Many of them go for long distances through the rice fields, where they cannot be covered by observation and serve

I believe they have done this very thing

no useful purpose other than a symbolic one. This may be all right in areas which are reasonably secure, provided that no materials in short supply, such as barbed wire and pickets, are wasted on them. Where, however, it is considered essential to have barbed wire and pickets for the defence of a strategic hamlet, then, even in the yellow areas, its length should not be more than four kilometres.* In the blue areas this should be reduced to three kilometres, and in the red areas to two to two and a half kilometres. These lengths might be increased where there is a larger number of houses inside the hamlet than is normal: for example, round a district town or a larger village. I am not suggesting that any of those which have already been constructed should be changed, but an effort should be made to reduce the size of the perimeter in future hamlets, particularly where these imported and scarce materials are being used. This will require that a greater number of houses should be regrouped inside. It is far better to adopt a firm policy and to do this now, thereby achieving an effective result, rather than finding that it has to be done later, after the Viet Cong have proved that such long fences provide no protection. Moreover, in any hamlet where even one house has to be regrouped, it is psychologically just as easy to regroup fifty. The individual does not feel so aggrieved if others are in the same position as himself.

From the security point of view, strategic hamlets should not only serve the purpose of protecting the inhabitants, but should also, where possible, be used to assist in the general security of an area, particularly in the protection of communications. Important road and railway bridges adjacent to a hamlet should be included within the hamlet defences. This can often be achieved where houses have to be regrouped by siting the new houses in such a position that they help to surround the bridge which needs protection. This is particularly important in an area where a battle with the Viet Cong for control of the area is under way. The blowing of a bridge may well lose the government ground access to the area for several days, thereby jeopardizing the defence of hamlets further along the road.

There has not always been proper co-ordination in the planning of strategic hamlets. For example, cases are occurring where elaborate defences are constructed but no men from the hamlet have been trained or armed to defend it. The first three essential ingredients are defences, trained men and an alarm and com-

* Yellow areas (also A) = government-controlled; blue areas (also B) = disputed; and red areas (also C) = Viet Cong–controlled.

munications system. As far as possible these should be provided simultaneously.

Generally there is less regrouping required in the rich and well-developed rice-field areas of the Delta than in the villages of the coastal provinces in Central Vietnam and those to the east and north of Saigon along the jungle fringes in Phuoc Tuy, Bien Hoa, Binh Duong and Tay Ninh Provinces, where the soil is not as fertile as in the Delta. In order to bring home to the people of these less fertile areas the advantages of the strategic hamlet, it is important that they should receive priority in those measures which are designed to increase production and material well-being, such as subsidized fertilisers, poison for rat control, improved livestock (including pigs, chickens and ducks), better seeds and fruit trees. We must demonstrate that strategic hamlets provide not only protection but increased prosperity.

I have already mentioned the need to stimulate production, particularly in strategic hamlets in the poorer provinces. As security improves, every effort should be made to stimulate trade and commerce so that people have more things to buy. At the same time, people should be encouraged to smarten their houses, hamlets and district towns so that a sense of order and well-being prevails. Prizes might be offered for the best kept hamlet in each district. Clean streets, some whitewash on the houses, replacement of thatch with tiles, all help to give an added sense of security, prosperity and good government. The government itself should set an example in smartening up its public buildings and compounds. This requires partly that province and district chiefs must start to think as much of the civilian aspect of their work as of the military. As soon as the security situation in any district or province is sufficiently improved, I feel certain that this attitude would be encouraged if military officers performing civilian functions wore civilian clothes.

The advance continued, and at the end of a further six months, in March 1963, I again reported to President Diem, in the following terms:

In the first year of the strategic hamlet programme, the main emphasis has been on those areas which represent the basic infra-structure of the country and which have been the easiest areas in which to start, i.e. along main roads and canals and round district and provincial capitals. From province to province these areas have automatically linked together and have provided the government with a firm base from which to continue the programme.

There is no doubt that the momentum of the programme can be maintained. This is important in order to keep the initiative and to compel the Viet Cong to use their forces to try to hold on to what they still control, thereby preventing them from infiltrating back into well-established strategic hamlets. It is, however, more important that the momentum should be maintained in the right pattern and in the right direction. In this respect we should no longer be too concerned with monthly statistics of hamlets completed, or with target dates which tend to encourage hasty and haphazard construction.

In the Delta area in the next stage it is vital that the major effort should be put into cleaning out the pockets and salients still under Viet Cong control in the developed and heavily populated areas before tackling the remoter areas and those which surround the Viet Cong war zones. If we try to go too fast by extending into the red areas, leaving pockets and salients of Viet Cong behind, we run the grave risk of overreaching ourselves and overcommitting the forces available. Hamlets in the red areas will require garrisons of Dan Ve, Bao An or, in some cases, even ARVN for a long period before reliable village militia can be raised to defend them.* If pockets and salients have been left behind, we will still be vulnerable in the rear at the same time, and our forces will become, as a result, too dispersed. At this point the Viet Cong, who will do everything to maintain the striking power of their regular units, will be able to launch damaging attacks against the government's scattered units. Simultaneously, even well-established hamlets in secure areas will remain vulnerable to subversion and reinfiltration from Viet Cong pockets in their neighbourhood. (I stressed the dangers of such subversion in my last report and the need to check and re-check against treachery from within.) A two-pronged counter-attack by the Viet Cong in this manner could seriously damage, if not demolish, the whole security framework created by the strategic hamlet programme.

The pockets and salients must be dealt with first for the following four main reasons:

(1) It will increase the security of established strategic hamlets and of the main populated areas and lines of communication.

(2) It will remove all threats to the rear, and will enable us to

* Dan Ve = Self-Defence Corps (a full-time paid Home Guard); Bao An = Civil Guard (a rural constabulary organized in companies); and ARVN = the regular army.

face the Viet Cong more or less on one front, which can then be steadily advanced towards their jungle bases.

(3) This in turn will enable us to release forces from the rear and to increase pressure on the front.

(4) It will force groups of defeated Viet Cong evicted from these areas (who do not surrender) to withdraw towards the main Viet Cong war zones, carrying with them an infectious low morale and increasing their supply problems.

Whereas it has been satisfactory in the first stage, during 1962, for the strategic hamlet programme to be planned at the province level, it is now important that its planned advance should be linked to the overall strategy. This requires that the planning of where and when strategic hamlets are to be established should be undertaken either at Tactical Zone or Corps level.

I wish to stress that the pockets and salients remaining under Viet Cong control are the hard core of their 'popular bases', and that these bases are far more important to them than any of their installations in war zones such as the Maquis D.* Nevertheless, if forces are available, every effort should still be made to keep the regular units of the Viet Cong in their war zones dispersed and on the move. Any caches of food supplies or other materials which can be found should be destroyed, together with any crops in remote areas that are obviously grown for Viet Cong consumption. We should aim, by the end of this year, to regain control of all the densely populated areas, and to force the Viet Cong regular units to remain dispersed in their war zones in order to feed off the scattered population not yet under our control or off their own cultivated plots.

No strategic hamlet is ever finished, and improvements should continually be taking place, both in the defence organization and in social and economic benefits. With assistance in providing schools, dispensaries, markets etc., this programme is going well, and I was impressed by the impact which the provision of electric light had made in one or two large hamlets. In some areas water is a major problem, particularly during the dry period. There is an opportunity here, where the number of houses warrants it, for a self-help project in the provision of water supplies. In hamlets on high ground where the water table is very low, there is normally some point close to the rice fields where a higher water table can be found. If a group of wells is dug at this point, the water from

* An extensive jungle area starting about 25 miles north-west of Saigon.

them can be pumped to a concrete tank at the highest point in the hamlet. From this tank a pipe can be run along the length of the hamlet, with stand pipes at regular intervals. The provision of such amenities is something the communists cannot match, and makes for very good publicity—quite apart from the benefit which it provides for the inhabitants.

It is most important to watch the incidence of Viet Cong activity in the neighbourhood of established strategic hamlets. If there is little or no activity where activity is to be expected, then it can be assumed that the Viet Cong have been able to maintain their contacts in nearby strategic hamlets and do not wish to draw attention to themselves. One of the criteria in assessing whether the Viet Cong still have contacts is whether or not young men are still being recruited from the area. If there is plenty of activity, then it means that the strategic hamlets are beginning to work well and the Viet Cong are being forced to react against them. They may hope by their activity to induce the government into taking sterner measures against the inhabitants. Manoeuvres such as this will be tried by the Viet Cong to maintain their contacts with the inhabitants and to subvert the hamlets. This calls for a very careful assessment by provincial and district intelligence officers, so that the government in turn does not make mistakes and play into Viet Cong hands.

Just as the application of control measures should be flexible, so should the organization of village militia. There is no guiding rule on this, such as the arming of a fixed number in each hamlet. Where the people are reliable and can be trusted, then the number of persons armed should be sufficient to defend the hamlet. Where the people are not yet to be trusted, then no one should be armed, and Dan Ve or Bao An will have to be used for the defence of the hamlet. There can be no half-way measures where the people are only partly trusted. This will only lead to treachery and disaster.

I can appreciate the need for some well-defended outposts in areas which are not yet under government control in order to maintain the government presence there and to obstruct the Viet Cong freedom of movement. Where, however, strategic hamlets are established, then all small posts outside the strategic hamlets should be demolished. They only provide the Viet Cong with an easy target which can be attacked without involving any inhabitants in the strategic hamlets, and add nothing to the security of the area. The Dan Ve or Bao An so released by this measure can be used either to increase the defences of the strategic hamlets or for active patrolling and ambushing in the area. This will have far more advantage and effect than these small posts, which are a death trap to their occupants. I personally would rather sleep on the open ground, even in wet weather, than in a small concrete or brick watch tower: rheumatism is preferable to death!

It will be seen from these excerpts of reports to President Diem that, in the first year of the programme, very considerable progress had been made, but that so far there had been a negligible Viet Cong reaction. The first cracks were, however, beginning to show, in that the programme was becoming overextended and Viet Cong pockets were being left behind as a constant threat to areas which otherwise should have been secured. This was not yet too serious and could have been rectified. Two things, however, happened in the summer of 1963 which had a major effect on the programme's future success. The first was the clash between the Ngo regime and the Buddhists. This led to an increasingly unstable political situation, in which the main issues of the war were forgotten or obscured. It also led to an emotional 'confrontation' between the regime and the American administration, with threats of the withdrawal or reduction of aid. This particularly affected Ngo Dinh Nhu, who was responsible for the strategic hamlet programme. He even went so far as to sack province chiefs who were co-operative towards the Americans, and pressed on regardless with the programme, in the hope of achieving a quick victory which would justify all the regime's policies and at the same time reduce its dependence on American aid.

The second was a more positive Viet Cong reaction to the programme. During the first year the Viet Cong had confined themselves to four lines of action: the issuing of continual propaganda against the strategic hamlets as 'concentration camps'; the penetration of the hamlets by their agents and supporters; the maintenance of pockets and salients under their own control; and the preservation of their regular units, which were rarely committed to a major action during this period. From July 1963 onwards, however, they started their attack on strategic hamlets, particularly those which were being hastily created under Ngo Dinh Nhu's accelerated programme. Fences were torn down; government construction work was destroyed and the inhabitants forced to return to their previous sites. Hamlet militia posts were constantly attacked and many weapons were lost. There were increased attacks on communications, such as mining of roads, in order to break government contact with the more isolated hamlets.

In September 1963 I reported to President Diem that the strategic hamlet programme had now gone too fast, with a consequent dispersal of effort and a scattering of hamlets over too wide an area. The figures speak for themselves:

Month	Total completed hamlets	Monthly increase
July 1962	2,559	—
August 1962	2,661	102
September 1962	3,089	428
October 1962	3,225	136
November 1962	3,550	325
December 1962	4,080	530
January 1963	4,441	361
February 1963	5,049	608
March 1963	5,332	283
April 1963	5,787	455
May 1963	6,226	439
June 1963	6,872	646
July 1963	7,220	348
August 1963	8,095	875

I told him that as a result of this haste, and because there had been no clear strategic direction of the programme, we were in a situation in which the available provincial forces were overextended, the Viet Cong had been presented with a number of soft and vulnerable targets and the government had been unable to achieve any really secure base areas. In many provinces the situation was serious, though not yet dangerous. It could still be restored and progress maintained. The requirement was a very clear decision on priority areas, and the consolidation of hamlets in both the first priority areas and the more secure areas. This required that resources be correspondingly allocated, and that a halt be called to the programme in the low priority areas. I also stressed the need for co-ordination between the military and the civil effort within each province, but more particularly between provinces. There was a tendency for each province chief to think that he was fighting a separate war. Army support for the programme had also been half-hearted. A battalion might be allocated to help clear a particular area, but would be withdrawn after two or three weeks, just at the critical period when the hold operation began, leaving the para-military forces to bear the brunt of the Viet Cong reaction. I complained, too, that even where the strategic hamlet programme had been more or less successfully completed, no start had been made in imposing resources control (see Chapter 12). I pointed out that there was no reason at all why we should continue to allow the Viet Cong to make use of trucks, buses, Lambrettas and boats for the movement of agents and couriers, or to use the main communications system of the country for obtaining supplies. These strictures were too late, and were lost in the prevailing political circumstances which led to the downfall of the regime in the *coup d'état* of November 1, 1963.

This was the final blow to the strategic hamlet programme. Those who succeeded President Diem had no prepared policy and delayed too long before taking any firm decisions. Province chiefs and other local officials were all changed in the next few months, some as many as three times, and in one instance four times. The Viet Cong took full advantage of the situation, and only the hamlets which had been well constructed and organized under the better province chiefs in 1962 were able to withstand the pressure for any length of time.

To reactivate such a programme in 1964 proved immensely difficult. There was neither the will nor the capacity in the government to put it through steadily and methodically. Successive weak and unstable governments, lacking an effective administrative machine as a result of the witch-hunt of all top officials in the post-Diem period, were understandably reluctant to take the tough and unpopular decisions necessary to save the situation; nor could the people themselves be expected to accept the effort required of them to do a second time what had already failed them once. As a result of the collapse of the programme, many of the local leaders in the rural areas were discredited or killed by the Viet Cong, and, in the absence of overwhelming support from and confidence in the government, others could hardly be expected to take their place.

Consequently, throughout 1964 there was a steady loss of population in the rural areas to the Viet Cong, and by the end of the year the villages were beginning 'to encircle the towns'.

Chapter 12

The Isolation of the Guerilla

AS we have seen, the major weakness in the Vietnamese implementation of the strategic hamlet programme was that it had no strategic direction, with the result that strategic hamlets were created haphazardly all over the country, and in no area was there a really solid block of them. This led to a situation where, instead of the hamlets on the perimeter of the advance forming the front line against the Viet Cong, almost every single hamlet was itself still in the front line and vulnerable to Viet Cong attack. The second weakness was that military operations, particularly in the Mekong Delta, were not designed to support the advance of the strategic hamlet programme. The third weakness was that no real effort was made to separate the population in the strategic hamlets from the Viet Cong by eliminating their agents and supporters inside the hamlets, or by imposing controls on the movement of people and supplies. Even if some more overt Viet Cong agents and supporters moved out of a strategic hamlet at the time when it was established, they subsequently had no difficulty in re-penetrating the hamlet, continuing subversion and maintaining their organization and infrastructure.

Basically, the Vietnamese seemed unable to understand that the establishment of strategic hamlets would accomplish nothing unless the other necessary measures were taken to achieve their three objects: of protection, of uniting and involving the people, and of development, with the ultimate aim of isolating the guerilla units from the population. Not only with regard to strategic hamlets but in other fields as well, the Vietnamese tended to confuse the means with the end. It took over three years to establish 500 defended Chinese villages in Malaya. In under two years in Vietnam over 8,000 strategic hamlets were created, the majority of them in the first nine months of 1963. No attention was paid to their purpose; their creation became the purpose in itself. A similar attitude prevailed with regard to defence posts. Hundreds of these had no function in the insurgency other than to defend themselves. This inability to think a thing through applied even to *coups d'état*. Governments could be overthrown with increasing frequency without previous thought as to what should replace them or what policies should be adopted.

The first step after the creation of a strategic hamlet is to create the conditions in which the population has the security to exercise the choice between supporting the insurgent forces and supporting the forces of the government. Strategic hamlets, firmly established and consolidated, built outwards from a secure base, armed for their own protection and supported by military or para-military forces to ensure the security of their outer perimeter and of their lateral communications with each other, can give the conditions which make it safe for a villager to decide to support the government against the insurgent. The two main practical measures here are the training and arming of the hamlet militia or home guard and the provision of a good communications system.

The hamlet militia in Vietnam were well trained and armed with carbines and shotguns, but they suffered from the same faults as the strategic hamlet programme. Too often they were exposed to attacks by insurgent units with which they could not be expected to cope. They were on full-time duty with little or no pay. This imposed an impossible strain on a peasant family. The real fault here lay in the fact that there was no established and territorially based government force, such as the police force in Malaya, to which they could look for orders and support or for which they could act as a local reinforcement. There were about 250,000 Home Guards in Malaya, but seldom, if ever, were more than 40,000–50,000 on duty and armed at any one time. In each village there was a police post, and the police officer in charge of the post, in accordance with either his instructions or the needs of the situation, could call on perhaps ten Home Guards one night, and five the next or even none at all, out of a total of fifty in the village. This flexible use of the volunteers enabled a much larger proportion of the population to be involved without preventing them earning their living. It also enabled all the necessary tasks to be done, including, if required, the call-up of the total number for a special operation. In Vietnam the system was far too rigid, and squads of up to thirty from one hamlet (always composed of the same men) were on full-time duty without the supervision and direction of a superior organization to ensure that they carried out their tasks properly. Even so, they did their best, and over 150,000 volunteered. Although there were some defections and disasters, the vast majority fought valiantly and suffered heavy casualties.

It was basically this failure to dovetail together the variety of para-military forces in Vietnam which made it almost impossible to consolidate the security framework. Roles and tasks were never clearly defined, and the most economical and effective use of the forces available could never be achieved.

If this applied to the operations aspect, it applied still more to intelligence, particularly the intelligence required to eliminate agents and supporters within the hamlet, without which full security could never be attained.

Security by itself is not enough to make the peasant willingly choose to support the government. Without it he cannot, even with it he still may not. The next step, therefore, is to influence his choice, which must still remain a free choice. He can only be made to choose freely to support the government if the government can show him that what it has to offer is something better than the insurgent can offer him. The importance of improving the standard of living of the peasants socially, politically, economically and culturally as a war measure has already been stressed. It is comparatively easy to accomplish in the more secure base areas and should follow in the less secure areas as the clear-and-hold operations take effect. It is important to get across that the benefits are a reward and a consequence of security, not a bribe. They serve as an example of what can be achieved when peace is restored.

There comes a point in the campaign at which, in order to achieve complete security, tougher measures are required, both to eliminate the insurgent organization within the hamlets and to create a greater physical barrier between the population and the guerilla units. If the foundation of the government's approach and the basis of its policy appeal to the peasant have been made clear, then these tougher measures to achieve victory are made much easier. The government must show that it is not only determined, but prepared, to be ruthless. This can best be explained by quoting a few examples of what may be necessary. In bad areas in which strategic hamlets are constructed, it may be necessary that no house should be left outside the perimeter, and all the inhabitants should be persuaded, even compelled if necessary, to move their houses inside. There should be no reluctance or hesitation about arresting insurgent agents or supporters. If a hamlet is overrun and the fence destroyed, it should be immediately repaired. If roads in the vicinity of a hamlet are cut, all the population should be turned out to repair them. Strict control over the movement of people and supplies should be enforced.

As a basis for these measures the first requirement is an identity card system throughout the country, covering all persons preferably down to the age of 12. (A communist subversive organization makes a tremendous use of teenagers, both boys and girls, as couriers and spies.) A list of the occupants of a house, together with their photographs, should be maintained in each house, with a copy at village or district headquarters. This makes it easy to check absentees and visitors. Areas where there is no habitation or cultivation should be declared prohibited areas. Dusk-to-dawn curfews outside hamlets should be imposed and strictly enforced. In bad areas it may even be necessary to impose curfews within the hamlet for certain periods of the night. Bulk supplies of food and other articles of value to the insurgents should be convoyed between towns and villages, and no individual should be allowed to take such articles outside the hamlet. In areas where a really strict control is required, rice may have to be distributed on a ration basis or already cooked (it then goes sour within two or three days), and canned goods should be punctured by the shopkeeper as they are sold. Check points should be established to enforce all these regulations, and snap checks should be carried out on all roads, rivers and tracks.

It has to be accepted that money is no great problem to an

insurgent movement. Half-starved terrorists were frequently
killed or captured in Malaya with wads of notes on them. The
two major sources of cash are local taxation on crops and
produce in insurgent-controlled areas, and protection money
levied on companies and businessmen who wish to avoid the
destruction, of or damage to their property. For example,
French-owned rubber estates in Vietnam continued to operate
even in bad areas, but they paid for it. Planters were frequently
kidnapped, and well treated, until payments were forthcoming.
They were then released. Bus and transportation companies
were a rich source of revenue, and in 1964 all cars travelling
on roads outside Saigon were charged £5 a month. A receipt
was given, and acted as a passport if the car was subsequently
stopped by the Viet Cong. When a village about fifteen miles
west of Saigon was recovered by the government in 1963, I
was surprised to notice quite a few fit and well-fed racing
ponies. On enquiry I learnt that they had been raced in
Saigon every week-end. It would have been interesting to
investigate their form. I am sure that the Viet Cong had no
difficulty in fixing the results of races and in bringing off a
number of successful betting coups. There is not a great deal
that the government can do to control the supply of money,
except to issue new currency notes at short notice and to give
very little time for old notes to be exchanged without an
investigation of their source. The emphasis of the government
control measures must be on the supplies which money can
buy.

Within a very short time the measures previously mentioned
will start to put the pressure on any guerilla units still remaining in the operational area, and foraging for supplies will
become their first priority. In spite of the measures, however,
some supplies will continue to leak out. In Malaya, rice was
carried out of villages inside bicycle pumps, in cigarette tins
and in false bottoms to buckets of pig-swill. Just as the government is putting the pressure on in this way, so the insurgent
must put the pressure on his supporters to continue smuggling
supplies. These supporters will be of two types: those who are
willing to help and those who have been forced to help. At this
point a good psychological line to take with the latter is that

they now have an excuse to refuse further assistance. They can complain to the insurgents when they encounter them outside the hamlet that the controls are rigidly enforced and that the risks are too great. This approach worked very well in Malaya and gave the enforced insurgent supporter his let-out. The argument was too strong for the insurgent to take any type of terrorist reprisal. This meant that a greater effort was required of the willing supporters, who therefore had to take greater risks in avoiding the controls. This helped to reveal their identity and, when caught red-handed, many of them rapidly realized their predicament and preferred the alternative of continuing to smuggle supplies and informing the authorities when and where they would be picked up.

There are many who will criticize the harshness of the measures which may have to be used. This is a mistaken attitude. What the peasant wants to know is: Does the government mean to win the war? Because if not, he will have to support the insurgent. The government must show it is determined to win. Only in that way will it instil the confidence that it is going to win. (It is interesting to recall that every order of the day issued by Vo Nguyen Giap in the period preceding and during the battle of Dien Bien Phu ended with the words 'With affection and determination to win'.) People will stand very harsh measures indeed, provided that they are strictly enforced and fairly applied to all, are effective in achieving their purpose and are seen to be so. The blame for the harshness of the measures can be placed squarely on the insurgent, and it should be made absolutely clear that as soon as the area is 'white', restrictions can gradually be withdrawn. There should be in the whole of the government's approach an adroit and judicious mixture of ruthlessness and sympathy. Where is the dividing line? The dividing line must be drawn at the point at which the government is in a position to give the peasant a clear choice between supporting the government or supporting the insurgent. In other words, when the government moves back into an area, saturates it, builds strategic hamlets, organizes their defence, provides social benefits and imposes measures which give the peasant an excuse not to support the insurgent, then the peasant has his choice, and the government must be ruthless in requiring him to make it. When, however, an area is outside government control and the peasant is at the mercy of the insurgent, then he has no choice, and the government has no right to be ruthless. There was a tendency in Vietnam to get this the wrong way round.

As an example of a ruthless measure it is worth quoting the case of a village in Malaya (Jenderam) of about 3,000 inhabitants. This was a very bad area, and the village itself was a centre of support and supply for a large unit of communist terrorists when most of the other surrounding areas had been cleared. Having given the inhabitants a choice between the government and the communists, and having failed to make any headway by appealing to or persuading them to co-operate, the government surrounded it with several battalions at dawn one morning and moved the whole village out. Everyone in it—men, women and children—went into detention. All the houses were razed to the ground and crops destroyed. This did not cause a public outcry because the effectiveness of the result, by leading to the elimination of the communist terrorist unit concerned, silenced all criticism. When the area was finally cleared of terrorists, the people were allowed to return, and the restoration of the village was then heavily subsidized by the government. It is now both peaceful and prosperous, but at the time when the action was taken, it showed everyone that the government was determined to win the war even if methods such as this had to be employed.

Measures of this nature cannot be effective unless there is an absolutely solid block of country under government control which has been cleared and held so that the insurgent has no means of either re-penetrating or bypassing it. When this has been achieved, the insurgent units which formerly operated in the area must fall back on the remaining areas still under insurgent control. Such areas are the 'popular bases' of the insurgent, where he has been longest in control and where the people have been completely dominated for many years. (These areas were quite easy to define both in Malaya and in Vietnam from the previous history of the Japanese occupation and the Viet Minh war.) This fall-back of guerilla units has a dual effect on the insurgent. First, more units have to be fed and supplied in a limited area, which imposes a greater logistic strain on the popular bases. Second, these units carry with them an air of despondency and defeat which is infectious. This is the moment when the government's surrender campaign should be going full blast.

Depending on the degree of insurgency in a country, it may take the government two, three or even four years to reach the state when its main base areas are white, when the previously disputed areas are fully under government control and when the insurgent is more or less confined to his popular base areas, which are probably scattered throughout the country close to jungle fringes and swamps. Even if the insurgent has not fought seriously for any of the disputed areas, he must now fight for his popular bases. These become the anvil of the battle. In these areas the government's technique is exactly the same, except that the prospects of raising reliable hamlet militia are probably remote. This means that full-time para-military forces must be employed on hamlet defence, and that the army, as well as clearing, must play a leading part in the hold period of the operation, including the enforcement of control measures. Even though forces will have been released from the white areas, there still may not be enough to deal with all the popular bases simultaneously, and there must be a careful selection of the sequence in which they will be dealt with. Normally it would be advisable to take first those which still impose a threat to the security or economy of the country, and to leave the remoter areas which impose little threat until last.

This period of the insurgency can well last two years or even more. It is the period when the regular units of the insurgents are gradually decimated by a process of attrition. Even so, the hard core will not be completely defeated and will tend to disperse and scatter into smaller, hard-hitting groups which can still do a great deal of damage. The period may be followed by overtures for peace, as in Malaya, and the government must steel itself and the people to finish the job off.

When the insurgents have been more or less completely

evicted from the populated and developed areas, they will finally fall back on the mountains, jungles and swamps, and it is in this sort of terrain that the dreary process of mopping-up will have to be carried out.]

Chapter 13

Jungle and Frontiers

IT is now time to consider what has been happening in the
mountains and jungles during the insurgency, and what the
government's policy should have been in preparation for the
period when the remaining insurgent forces retreat to their
jungle bases. The first problem is the government's policy
towards the aboriginal hill tribes who inhabit the jungles, and
the second problem is that of control over frontiers which run
through such areas.

The aboriginal hill tribes in Malaya numbered about 50,000,
whereas in Vietnam they were spread over a much vaster area
and number well over 600,000. These ethnic minorities represent people who were among the earliest immigrants in pas-
sage to south-east Asia. Groups of them got left behind in
countries *en route*, and were subsequently forced back into the
mountains and jungles of those countries by stronger successive
invaders. As a result, there is in them a natural latent hostility
and suspicion, common to all hill people, towards the people
of the plains, and in character they are simple, shy and nervous
with strangers. In so far as they were contacted and befriended
during the period of colonial rule, the greatest success was
most often achieved by the eccentric European with a vocation
for making the study of such people his life-long work and
interest. The majority of tribes are nomadic agriculturalists,
cutting down several acres of jungle to grow crops for two or
three years and then moving on to another area. Their existence is eked out by a little fishing and hunting with crossbow
or blowpipe. Each tribe, however, maintains itself as a separate
entity within well-defined boundaries and regards the jungle
area in which it lives as its own by custom and right. Some,
of course, have had a closer contact with the outside world and
have achieved a higher degree of sophistication than the
remoter tribes.

The Japanese occupation, and in Vietnam the Viet Minh

war, brought all the tribes into much closer contact with
people from outside, and they were used by guerilla and
resistance forces both as a source of food and for the provision
of porters. Both the communist terrorists in Malaya and the
Viet Cong in Vietnam maintained these relationships, and
developed a very strong organization for retaining the good-
will and the support of the hill tribes. Their importance lay in
the fact that they inhabited the main mountain ranges, which
were the spinal column of both countries, and the frontier
jungle areas between Malaya and Thailand and between
Vietnam and Southern Laos.

In their policies towards the hill tribes the governments of
both Malaya and Vietnam were faced with two identical
problems. The first was the long-term problem of assimilating
the hill tribes and raising their standard of living so that they
could play a part in the future of the country. In carrying out
this policy, the government, while recognizing the claims of
the tribes to their particular areas, must encourage them to
develop a more static and productive form of agriculture and
must bring them some of the benefits of good government in
the way of schools and medical attention. One of the reasons
why the tribes have to be persuaded to abandon their nomadic
form of agriculture is to reduce hillside erosion, which causes
the silting up and flooding of rivers in the plains. But the main
reason is the shortage of land in the plains, with the need to
open up new areas of cultivation in the highlands for the
surplus population. Such land should be taken from tribal
areas only with the agreement of the tribe, and this may
require a long period of persuasion. The second problem
facing the government is, of course, to woo the hill tribes away
from the insurgents, with whom they have been in close contact, to the side of the government, with which in the past
they have had little contact. Both these problems have to be
faced simultaneously, though it has to be recognized that the
first may take a generation to solve.

The government is likely to be helped with the insurgent
problem by the fact that when the insurgency breaks out, the
insurgents themselves need considerable assistance from the
hill tribes in the provision of food and porters. The easiest

way, though it may take time, to move insurgent forces from one area in the country to another is over the mountain trails. Logistic support for this movement soon puts a considerable strain on the tribal economy, and the first sign that this is happening is an exodus of tribal groups, in an impoverished and starving state, seeking the assistance of the government. This is a state of affairs of which the government must take full advantage, whatever the situation may be in the rest of the country. The great difficulty here is that it is not desirable to resettle these groups either away from their tribal areas or in close proximity to civilization, such as on the outskirts of a village or town. It is a fact that this latter measure has a deteriorating effect both morally, in that tribal customs are broken down, and physically, in that the tribe starts to die off, lacking as it does any immunity to 'civilized' diseases. Nor is it wise to encourage a wholesale exodus. Apart from the immense administrative problems that this would pose at a difficult stage in an insurgency, it is not desirable to empty the jungle, leaving it entirely in insurgent hands.

It should be the aim of the government at this stage to make a good impact on the hill tribes by giving assistance to the refugees, and by encouraging refugee groups to return to their tribal areas as soon as protection can be afforded. It is through the refugee groups' contacts with those members of the tribes still remaining in the jungle that the government can obtain intelligence on insurgent training camps and supply dumps in the jungle areas. The methods of providing protection, as the refugees are encouraged to return to their areas, are very similar to those relating to strategic hamlets. An accessible base area should be selected as a focal point for a group of tribal villages. It should then be the role of the special forces to enlist all able-bodied men in the area to act as scouts and to give warning of any insurgent movement, and from this group to select the best to form an armed strike force, which may vary in size from fifty to two hundred men, for the defence of the area. Once such a base has been established and is working well, the aim should then be to extend out to further villages in the same tribal area. It is, however, in my view most important to get the timing right for the establishment of such base areas, because if they are established too soon, while the insurgent is still in control of villages in the foothills outside the jungle, the base areas themselves will be extremely vulnerable. They should not therefore be established until the government is certain that it is in the process of regaining control in the foothills. Tribal strike forces cannot be expected to withstand attacks or to protect villages from insurgent units of battalion strength. If they are established prematurely, it will only lead to disaster, and as a result the government may lose any control or support which it has laboriously built up in the tribal areas. If, however, the strike forces are established to coincide with the phase when the insurgents have been driven out of the plains back into the jungle and are dispersed and operating in small parties, then the strike forces are ideal for joining in the hunt and for helping to control the frontier in the closing stages of an insurgency. A small aboriginal force in Malaya (the Senoi Pra'ak), numbering not more than three hundred, accounted for more terrorists killed in the last two years of the Malayan Emergency than all the rest of the security forces put together.

If the government waits until this stage is reached, it will then also be in a position to establish secure 'forts' in the deep jungle areas, which can operate both as patrol bases and as administrative centres for the aboriginal tribes. In addition to providing local security, the government can build schools and clinics and establish trading posts. If the sites are well selected, it is around these forts that the government can demonstrate improved methods of agriculture and gradually encourage a more settled way of life for the tribes. If there is also an international frontier which the insurgents have been crossing, their final remnants will gradually retreat from the jungle across this border, and the government should maintain its small aboriginal units to act as a continual frontier screen, working to the forts situated at some depth, well back from the frontier.

In some parts of Malaya the insurgent forces retreated back into the swamp jungles of the plains, which were uninhabited by any aboriginal tribes. In these areas the mopping-up process was considerably more difficult, and large numbers of troops had to be used to hunt down very small parties of insurgents. There was one case when three battalions spent over two months in a large swamp jungle trying to eliminate without contact the four remaining terrorists in Selangor State, out of an original total of over two thousand. It was decided to call the whole operation off and to leave the party to be picked up later through contacts in the neighbouring villages. On the last day of the operation, the four terrorists walked into a small ambush, as a result of which three of them were killed and the final one surrendered two days later.

Until the jungle mopping-up phase is reached, the government should limit its jungle operations to those of the long-range penetration type, in order not only to deny freedom of movement to the insurgents in the jungle, but to reduce the absorptive capacity of adjacent highland areas to infiltration from across the frontier. A long jungle frontier cannot be sealed off. It is a waste of time and resources to build forts, frontier roads or fences, all of which will tie down a large body of troops for no effective purpose. Nothing can prevent small parties of men crossing such a frontier at any time. The only real limitation on the number of infiltrators during the initial stages of an insurgency will be the ability of the insurgent organization to feed and maintain them during the long jungle marches that will have to be undertaken before they reach their final destination well inside the country. By long-range penetration operations, designed to deny freedom of movement or at least to slow it down, and by other operations, designed to purchase all surplus stocks of food in the frontier areas, the government can reduce the absorptive capacity of such areas so that infiltration, while it will remain a nuisance, cannot become a decisive factor in the campaign. Not only does the insurgent organization in the mountain jungle areas have to be fed, but every two hundred men passing through would themselves require at least five tons of rice (more in paddy form, i.e. unhusked) for every month of their journey. This logistic problem is the weak link in the infiltration chain and should be the government's initial target.

When resources later become available, the government can then, in preparation for the final stages of the campaign, consider the building of a road, preferably fifty miles back from the frontier, where it will also have greater development advantages in the future. This should become the government's main base line for control, with fingers stretching out towards the frontier by means of the 'forts' already mentioned, from which aboriginal border scouts can be supported. This will establish a border system of control by which the infiltrator, although he can still cross the frontier, should be spotted and picked up within a week, i.e. before he can reach his objective within the country.

If jungle operations are to achieve success, special training is, indeed, necessary, but not special men. Above all, the soldier has to become accustomed to living and moving in the jungle, and this takes time. Plainsmen and peasants of a country with large jungle areas have an ingrained, almost traditional, fear of the jungle, which only experience and training can eradicate. There are no natural jungle fighters. Even the insurgent has to learn it.

I have no intention of launching into a jungle training manual, and the only other point I wish to stress is the importance of rations. If men are reasonably fit and well-fed before they go in (and for a long session it may pay not to be too fit and to have a bit of surplus fat, a sort of camel's hump which can be worked off in the process of penetrating to the operational area), and are going to be well-fed again when they come out, their rations should be palatable and consist of what the men like, rather than what the nutrition experts consider good for them. I speak with some feeling on this point, having lived on American K rations for over three months. After two or three weeks it was impossible to eat the equivalent of more than one meal a day instead of the three provided. The lack of a satisfactory compact ration palatable to the Vietnamese was one of the limiting factors in jungle operations in Vietnam. This resulted in jungle operations being of too short a duration and, to make up for it, on too large a scale. Normal rations were carried, including live chickens on a pole. Guerillas are not going to be seen off by battalions marching into the jungle with transistors blaring and chickens clucking. It is more likely to be the other way round.

Chapter 14

The Advisory Role

JUST as within a country a communist insurgency cannot be dealt with in isolation, so, in a world-wide context, it is not an isolated event but an integral part of the continuing process of communist underground aggression by means of subversion and terror. No underdeveloped or newly independent country can face this threat alone. It will need more than political support from the free world. Economic and material support will certainly be necessary, and military support may be required in addition to military equipment. This poses immense political difficulties both for the country itself and for any supporting power.

The threatened country will quite rightly be most jealous about guarding its newest and most precious asset: its independent sovereignty. Conversely, the supporting power will not wish to be viewed, either in the threatened country or in the world in general, as imposing any form of control which could be interpreted as colonialism. But at the same time it must be recognized that any supporting power which is prepared to offer its blood, treasure and prestige must have some say in the conduct of events. No threatened country, in deference to its sovereignty, can expect to be allowed to squander these gifts recklessly. A formula needs to be found which will make the relationship a strong working partnership.

I think the answer must be a treaty, but not of course a treaty of protection in the old style, which in the modern context would be quite unacceptable to both parties politically, and quite impracticable to operate as a basis for a working partnership. Even in Malaya, where such treaties between the Sultans of the Malay States and the British Crown were still in existence at the time of the Emergency, it was essential to associate the representatives of the people of Malaya with all government policies by persuasion and without reference to the clause in the treaties which required that British advice must be accepted. This approach resulted in an excellent working relationship, which continued into the period after independence, when a new defence treaty between the independent Federation of Malaya and the United Kingdom was signed. It is this defence treaty which governs the relationship in the present period of confrontation with Indonesia. In Vietnam there was no treaty between the South Vietnamese government and the United States; there was only a much looser form of agreement, under which, to use the expression most often quoted, the United States 'would help the people of Vietnam to help themselves'. This is an admirable concept, but when it comes down to the day-to-day working relationship, it leaves far too many undefined gaps in the respective responsibilities and obligations.

The first advantage of a formal treaty is that it is made between two sovereign states, and that their respective sovereignties are recognized by the treaty itself. But the greater advantage is that, under a treaty, the arrangement by which the two parties will consult in order to reach agreement on joint policies, and will co-operate to carry out these policies, can be laid down. This must be a strictly formal arrangement, which should be rigidly adhered to. What I have in mind is that a joint War Council should be established, with appropriate representation for both parties, such as Ministers of the threatened country and the local heads of aid agencies of the supporting power, and that this Council should be served by a small joint secretariat. All major policy decisions which affect both parties must be put to this Council and approved. These should then be issued by the secretariat as directives and instructions to the government ministries, as well as to the supporting agencies, in order to ensure that they are distributed and followed right down the line. Progress on the implementation of the policies should be constantly reviewed, and modifications should be made, if necessary, by the Council —and not by anyone else. In the event of disagreement between the parties in the Council, the matter must then be submitted to the respective governments at Prime Minister–Ambassador level, so that agreement or compromise can be sought.

Obviously it is desirable that there should be good personal relationships between the respective counterparts at every level from the Head of the Government and the Ambassador of the supporting power downwards. Such personal relationships will be most readily established on a firm basis if respective responsibilities and obligations are formally defined, and, below War Council level, these can be laid down by the War Council itself to provide the necessary co-ordination in the implementation of policies at provincial and district levels. Personal relationships, however, should be used to grease the wheels of the War Council machinery, not to take over its functions. For example, if the Prime Minister and the Ambassador meet to discuss a certain line of policy and reach agreement, this agreement should then be processed through the War Council in order to ensure that it is issued as an instruction in the normal way and that all relevant details are tied up. If this is not done, and if action is taken on such an agreement by both parties through their own channels, there will be a lot of loose ends. Loose ends have a tendency to flap, and will flap their hardest at the end of the line where the policy has to be implemented on the ground.

Naturally the War Council does not want to become bogged down in too much detail, and, to avoid this, it should establish under itself committees for particular subjects, such as military operations, intelligence, psychological warfare, strategic hamlets and so on, or even for a single particularly crucial clear-and-hold operation. This will work well, provided that the committees adhere to the Council's directives and themselves issue their instructions through the joint secretariat.

A final advantage of these formal arrangements from the point of view of the supporting power is that it becomes identified with the national policies of the threatened country, and is supporting these policies, instead of becoming too much identified with individual personalities, with some of whose policies it may not wish to be associated.

The presence of a formal treaty and the joint machinery established under it will help the supporting power to solve the second main problem of its advisory role. This is that all advisers must speak with one voice, and that the provision of aid must be fully co-ordinated in furtherance of the main aim and in accordance with the agreed plan.

There are a number of human tendencies that have to be kept in check. Where personal relationships between the counterparts of two countries are exceptionally good, there will be a temptation to pour in extra aid, out of turn and not in accordance with the plan, because it will be thought that such additional aid will be more effectively used, and that the 'response' should be met. (This should not be confused with reinforcing success as part of a change of emphasis in any plan.) This switching of aid will serve only to throw plans and programmes out of balance, and cause more vital areas, where the response may not be so good, to lag further behind. The situation will be still more harmful if the adviser concerned has been lured into it by meeting questionable requests for aid in order to establish his good relations in the first place. If others follow this example, then the whole aid programme will be in real trouble, and a situation will develop in which everyone is fighting his own little war without regard to anyone else.

In this respect, heads of agencies must beware of their specialists. Many of these are likely to have a narrow view of the war as a whole and to be concerned only with their own pet project. They will press this forward in order to complete it within their tour of duty, quite irrespective of whether their action suits the particular phase in the campaign or makes any positive contribution to victory. I cannot subscribe to the view that it does not matter if, as a result of impatience, certain items of aid are distributed to areas under enemy control because 'they all have the clasped hands on them'.

There will certainly be a tendency, too, on the part of ministries and departments of the local government, to play one agency off against another. If you cannot get guns for your private army from one agency, you can try another. The mere threat of trying another may be sufficient. It works well enough internationally, so why not internally?

As a means of checking these tendencies and ensuring a co-ordinated effort, I am a firm believer in the appointment by the supporting power of a pro-consul with full local authority

over all policy and all agencies. This pro-consul must of course
be the Ambassador. This may raise problems of command
channels as between agencies locally (including military
headquarters) and their head offices in the capital of the
supporting power. The answer, briefly, is that all policy
questions must be routed through the Ambassador, and that
direct communication between agencies locally and their
headquarters should be confined to the administrative and
logistic measures necessary to give effect to approved policy.
What the pro-consul requires is full support and backing from
his government and, since most policy proposals will originate
at his end, fast decisions on them. What he does not require
are conflicting policy proposals from agency headquarters in
his capital and constant queries and requests for progress
reports suitable only for computer processing. The war can
be won only by those on the spot. Let them be trusted to get
on with it.

It must of course be assumed that the policy of providing
aid to a threatened country is the national policy of the
supporting power and will not be affected by a change of
government. Any possibility of that would be fatal to confidence. There are, however, other aspects where the domestic
policy of the supporting power may influence the degree and
form of aid and even the internal policies of the threatened
country when they are dependent on such aid. This is a
difficult problem, particularly since it may affect the timing
of particular lines of action. There is nearly always a psychological moment when a certain line of action within a threatened country may have its maximum good effect but may not
suit the domestic policy of the supporting power at that time
(because, for example, of imminent elections). There is no real
answer to this, except that the pros and cons have to be very
carefully weighed.

Another problem in this context, which continually arises
in the advisory role, is that while aid in many forms can be
injected into the threatened country, it does not follow that
ways of life can be simultaneously transferred to a totally
different environment. To expect this will merely frustrate
the adviser and cause resentment among the local officials

with whom he is dealing. It takes a long time to effect cultural and political changes, and the provision of aid, or the withholding of it, is not a suitable lever for forcing such reforms. It is essential, therefore, for the adviser to look at everything from the local point of view and not to expect that the provision of aid will do more than provide the very limited benefits for which it was intended. [He cannot expect that the threatened country will either organize itself or conduct its affairs on the same lines, or in accordance with the same standards, as those of the supporting power.] The real point here, which is all the adviser can hope for, is to get the local government to function effectively and at least to take the necessary action itself, even if it is done in its own traditional way.

The agencies of the supporting power must resist the temptation to take over some of these functions because they think they can do them better. If they give in to the temptation, they will be failing in their main task, which is to build up the administrative machinery of the local government and the experience of the individuals in it so that the local officials themselves perform their duties more effectively.

This, to my mind, is the real purpose of aid in all contexts including counter-insurgency: to help the local government to get its organization right and its departments working efficiently. Because of this, it is most important to give very careful consideration to both the forms and the volume of aid. Training is undoubtedly the first priority in both the military and the civilian fields. On the military side, standards, and the training courses to achieve them, are well established, and facilities are comparatively easy to provide, so that there is little reduction in the thoroughness of the training however great the expansion of the forces.

On the civilian side, however, there is a definite tendency to skimp the training and to indulge, in times of crisis, in crash programmes. This is a fatal mistake. Unless an effective administration is maintained and steadily improved by the recruitment and training of the best young men in the country, national policies become meaningless because, without the functioning of an effective administration, no policies can be carried out. This training requirement applies not only to administrative officers in the ministries and provinces but also to all the technical departments, such as education, health, agricultural services, the police force and so on. The training of professional officers and qualified technical assistants at all levels in the administration, to provide services and perform duties which are of direct benefit to the people, is far more important than constant crash programmes for the training of political and information cadres, who merely lecture the people in accordance with the whims of the particular government of the moment. If the training of the required officials is promoted during the subversive phase, and continued without interruption during the opening stages of the insurgency, then a steady supply will be available when the situation becomes critical. If, instead, because the demands are urgent, such training is reduced and short crash programmes are instituted in its place, there will merely be a constant supply of inexperienced and incompetent officials, who will be quite incapable of implementing the policies and measures required to defeat an insurgency, and who will merely add to the confusion.

The second form of aid which should be given priority is the improvement of the communication infrastructure of the country, including roads, bridges, airfields and radio networks. This is important not only in the counter-insurgency aspect, from the point of view of deployment of forces, but also in order to improve, even during the insurgency, the production potential and development of the rural areas of the country. This leads to the third priority, which is to increase the agricultural production of the country, with emphasis, during the insurgency, on the secured areas. This is far more important during an insurgency than the development of secondary industry. A 5 per cent increase in agricultural production will make a far greater impact on the economy of the country as a whole, and on the vital peasant element, than a 500 per cent increase in the production of manufactured goods.

Without the training of permanent officials and without the additional revenues from increased production, all attempts to improve the social services, as the fourth priority, will fail. It is easy enough to launch a major programme for the building of schools, hospitals, clinics etc., but, without the staff to man them or the revenue to support them, aid devoted to this purpose will be largely wasted. The same applies to the fifth priority, which embraces all the other minor projects of rural aid programmes in conjunction with clear-and-hold operations.

If the programme for the form which aid should take is tackled in this order, then the equally difficult problem of the volume of aid will be more easily solved. The supporting government must consider how far it should contribute to both the capital and the annually recurrent expenditure of the threatened country. [The less aid is given and the more the threatened country is compelled to rely on its own resources, the more effective the results will be.] For this reason the emphasis of aid should be on capital expenditure, and there should be a great reluctance to become involved in support of the budget of annually recurrent expenditure.

In the military field this is fairly straightforward and takes the form of equipment, weapons, transport, training establishments, barracks, airfields, naval bases and the like. In assessing the requirements, apart from military considerations, the supporting power must be particularly careful to take account of economic and financial factors and not to saddle the country with assets of this nature which it will not be able to maintain by itself within the foreseeable future. Similarly in the economic field the emphasis should be on capital expenditure designed to increase the productivity and revenue of the country. If too much emphasis is laid on social services, such as clinics and schools (which are costly to run without a corresponding increase in revenue producing schemes), the country will soon be in financial difficulties and will become permanently dependent on foreign aid to meet its recurrent expenditure. This does not mean that, at a time of insurgency, the supporting power should not contribute to the recurrent expenditure, but it is desirable to limit this contribution as far as possible. Malaya was fortunate in this respect in that the Korean war heavily inflated the prices of her primary products, such as tin and rubber, with the result that government revenue soared to such an extent that it could meet the costs of the Emergency and even build up surpluses over the critical period. Subsequently, when aid on annually recurrent expenditure was required from the British government, this was calculated in accordance with estimates of revenue and expenditure over a three-year period, but, on being granted, was not allocated to any particular item. This has its advantage in that the supporting power is not then identified with any specific government policy, not even the payment of the troops.

There is only a certain amount of aid, as I have mentioned earlier, which a country can absorb. Just as an insurgent movement has a limited absorptive capacity for outside assistance by way of infiltration, so has a threatened government in respect of aid. Even if aid projects seem highly desirable, as they always do to those who advocate them, there is a limit to what can be absorbed and achieved over a period of years without overloading either the administration or the economy. However tempting it may be to rush ahead, if foreign resources are available, this will only result in the whole government machine grinding to a halt. The receipt of aid should never become the primary function of government ministries and departments. Their primary function is to govern and administer the country, not to act as chain-stores for the retailing of foreign aid.

It follows from this that, if the situation deteriorates, then, as the insurgent movement and its capacity to absorb infiltration expands, so will the government's capacity to absorb aid decline. In these circumstances the supporting power must reduce aid which has to be channelled through the local government machine, and confine it to selected projects which can immediately affect the situation. This is not the time to think in terms of textile mills and oil refineries, which will only distract attention and resources from immediate essentials. At the same time, the supporting power will inevitably have to consider direct assistance, military or otherwise, which will not cause a diversion of local effort.

Much the same considerations apply in the more strictly advisory field, which, for obvious political reasons, is further complicated by the need on the military side to keep the presence of foreign military advisers to the minimum. If things are not going right, it is most unlikely that the solution will be found merely by increasing the quantity of advisers. This is liable to be counter-productive and can reach the point at which advice begins to revolve on a closed circuit. I think the weakness in Vietnam in this respect stemmed partly from the fact that American military personnel did such short tours. If unaccompanied by their families, tours were limited to one year. However high the calibre, and it was uniformly good, no great achievements in counter-insurgency are possible in such a short period. All that the individual can hope to do is to leave his post at the end of the year as he would like to find it. He cannot do more than prepare the ground for his successors. It was a great pity that the first group of advisers, who were allocated to the provinces in early 1962, were not able to do a second year and so provide continuity through this decisive period. Some means should have been found, such as giving them a month's home leave every five months, to make this possible.

It has to be accepted that the advisory role is naturally frustrating. As a result, there is a strong temptation to seek short cuts and distractions when the hard slog of clear-and-hold appears to be making little headway. There was a constant tendency in Vietnam to mount large-scale operations, which had little purpose or prospect of success, merely to indicate that something aggressive was being done. Coupled with this, there was a mounting reliance on air power, partly because it was a more familiar form of warfare, and partly because it was to a large extent under advisory control. Every field of activity needs to be carefully analyzed to ensure that, when the resources expended have been taken into account, it is contributing to the primary object of regaining control in the countryside. Distractions, however spectacular and attractive they can be made to appear if only as an experiment, which in fact merely increase the involvement and divert resources without improving the prospects, should be recognized for what they are.

Chapter 15

Feet on the Ground

IT is not within the scope of this book to chronicle recent events in Vietnam or to speculate on the prospects which lie ahead. But the situation as it developed in 1965, with the commitment of American combat troops on a large scale to the fighting within South Vietnam and the bombing of North Vietnam, must be considered in relation to the problems of counter-insurgency generally, irrespective of the particular outcome in Vietnam.

By the beginning of 1965, the Viet Cong had established a position in South Vietnam whereby they were in control of large areas of the countryside and had sufficiently penetrated the towns to create conditions of instability, which, in turn, were undermining the whole fabric of organized government. To add to this atmosphere of instability, there had been continual changes of government during the preceding few months. The two major threats which developed from this situation were, first, that the armed forces of South Vietnam might be defeated piecemeal and their morale broken, thereby destroying the physical base for continued resistance to the insurgent; and, second, that the government itself might completely collapse, thereby destroying any remaining political base.

In such circumstances, two further complicating factors will almost certainly arise. In view of the greatly expanded base of support for the insurgents in those areas of the countryside under their control, there will be a corresponding increase in the insurgent capacity to absorb further aid from outside. Whereas in the past this aid may have been limited to a continual flow of small parties of men and materials, the insurgent movement will now be in a position to absorb whole regular units and heavier weapons. Secondly, as soon as it becomes apparent that there is a danger of escalation, others will become alarmed by the situation and pressures will develop to effect a ceasefire and to end the war by negotiations. This will not appeal either to the insurgent, who can see victory on the ground within his grasp, or to the government, for whom the prospect of negotiations from a position of absolute weakness might be the last straw in breaking the morale of its own forces and eroding its own position.

This is the moment of decision for the supporting power, to whom it will be quite clear that the alternatives are either an outright victory for the insurgent and the complete submersion of a people who have been fighting valiantly over the past few years for their freedom and independence, or its own major involvement in the fighting. I doubt whether any supporting power which has both the resources and the resolution could, in such circumstances, fail to choose the second alternative.

When the supporting power becomes involved in this way, the positive initial aims of the government, and the supporting power, must inevitably be limited. The first immediate aim will be to secure the areas still held by the government, including the major towns and main centres of population. This in turn will mean that there must be still further contraction in the remoter areas of the countryside and that small towns and defended posts, which cannot be successfully relieved when attacked by superior guerilla forces, should be evacuated. This aim might be summed up as securing the enclaves. The second and equally important aim, from the point of view of the future, will be to stabilize the government within the enclaves and to reorganize it, together with its forces, for future operations to regain its lost territory. It would be a great mistake to go further than this and to assume that the application of military power in whatever form can turn defeat into early victory, because it must be recognized that much of the military power is irrelevant to the targets which are available. The overall aim at this stage is therefore no more than that of re-establishing within the country a firm base and a position from which it will be possible to return to the principles of counter-insurgency.

If a firm base is to be re-established, which brings us back to the fifth basic principle of counter-insurgency, and a situation is to be created in which there is some prospect of expanding the enclaves and regaining control over the countryside which has been lost, then the other four basic principles, and the organization and measures discussed in this book, will still apply. It will still be necessary, with the aid of a reformed intelligence organization, to make the political subversive organization of the insurgents the primary target, initially within the enclaves themselves. It will still be necessary to produce a co-ordinated plan for the recovery of the lost areas, to re-establish the rule of law and to maintain as the primary aim the rebuilding of the country so that it can once again become economically and politically stable and viable. This result cannot be achieved merely by the application of absolute force to the situation. It is just possible that force might achieve a temporary victory; but it would leave almost every single internal problem unsolved. You cannot win the game merely by changing the rules.

It may appear an alarming, if not a gloomy, prospect that all these processes have to be gone through a second time. But there will be a number of new advantages in the situation which will operate to the benefit of the government. First and foremost, the insurgents will have been robbed of their immediate expectation of victory and the momentum of their advance will have been lost. This will affect their morale and will tend to put them on the defensive in the areas under their control. At the same time the people in these areas will have had a taste of insurgent rule. Whereas during the guerilla phase of an insurgency the insurgents' control has been for limited purposes, when large areas come under their full control they will have had to accept more of the obligations of administration, and even government, for which they are likely to have been ill-prepared. It was a very significant feature of Vietnam that, where, during the Viet Minh war against the French, whole provinces were under Viet Minh administration, the people of these provinces in the subsequent war with the Viet Cong often provided the staunchest recruits for the government forces, particularly for the Self-Defence Corps in defence of their own villages. The province of Quang Ngai was an outstanding example of this. If, therefore, the government in its approach to the problem of regaining control in the countryside can establish a position whereby it can claim to be the liberator, it is likely to have a far greater success than it had in the past, when its approach was one of pacification. Finally, the pressure for negotiations will still be present. But if this has been delicately handled, the onus of accepting negotiations will fall on the insurgent, and this is a prospect for which he will find it difficult psychologically to prepare his supporters.

*   *   *

It should be clear that, when the build-up phase, the insurgency itself and the continuing threat of subversion after the insurgency have all been taken into account, the government and people of a threatened country, together with those members of the free world who support it, must be prepared to face a long, arduous and protracted struggle. The Emergency in Malaya lasted twelve years, and the insurgency in Vietnam has been going on for over six years with bitter intensity and no successful conclusion in sight. This cost in time may represent a very large slice out of individual lives, but in the life of a country it is a comparatively short span. There are many examples in history when countries have faced such turmoil for one or two generations and still triumphed over tyranny and aggression. The very nature of a communist-inspired insurgency, where force of arms alone will not prevail, dictates that a long-term view must be taken of all the problems which arise.

Progress cannot be judged by the success or failure of one short-term operation, nor by statistics even over a period of a year or more. For example, variations in the monthly incident rate can be deceptive. A drop in the number of incidents could mean that more areas are under insurgent control with no incidents reported in them. Conversely, when the government initiates action in an insurgent-controlled area or even a disputed area, the number of incidents can be expected to rise rapidly as the insurgents begin to react. Casualty figures also are a poor indication, even if they are accurate. A better guide is the capture and loss of weapons, although the government must be prepared for a heavier loss at the time when the hamlet militia are first armed, a time which should otherwise be regarded as a period of progress. The two best guides, which cannot readily be reduced to statistics or processed through a computer, are an improvement in intelligence voluntarily given by the population and a decrease in the insurgents' recruiting rate. Much can be learnt merely from the faces of the population in villages that are subject to clear-and-hold operations, if these are visited at regular intervals. Faces which at first are resigned and apathetic, or even sullen, six months or a year later are full of cheerful welcoming smiles. The people know who is winning.

It is important, therefore, not to make a crisis out of a setback (such as the Ap Bac battle in Vietnam in January 1963), or even a series of setbacks. There will certainly be mistakes, failures and defeats which, by the nature of guerilla warfare, appear as spectacular victories for the insurgent. These must be kept in perspective and set against steady but unspectacular progress in other fields. A guerilla ambush which wipes out a government company is more than offset by the recovery of several villages to the government side or the breaking up of an insurgent underground network in a district town. The government and its supporters must weather the shocks and keep their nerve. Confidence is the most precious ingredient for success, and it is the test of leadership to maintain course without wavering.

I remember, on coming out of church one Sunday in Saigon, drawing the attention of Mr Cabot Lodge, the American Ambassador, to the first lines of an American hymn which we had just sung:

> *Awake, my soul, stretch every nerve*
> *And press with vigor on.*

I suggested that that should be his motto. Subsequently, at an official luncheon in London in the late summer of 1964, he reminded me of this. I could not, on the spur of the moment, recollect the words of the second verse, which would have been most suitable to quote back to him on that occasion:

A cloud of witnesses around
Hold thee in full survey;
Forget the steps already trod
And onward urge thy way.

The three indispensable qualities in counter-insurgency are patience, determination and an offensive spirit, but the last should be tempered with discretion and should never be used to justify operations which are merely reckless or just plain stupid.

It is a persistently methodical approach and steady pressure which will gradually wear the insurgent down. The government must not allow itself to be diverted either by counter-moves on the part of the insurgent or by the critics on its own side who will be seeking a simpler and quicker solution. There are no short-cuts and no gimmicks. Even modern weaponry gives only a marginal advantage, because the guerillas will be armed mainly with captured government weapons.

The only two prerequisite and enduring assets are brains and feet. These are entirely human. The side which has its feet on the ground at the right time and in the right place will win.